Praying with
Process Theology

Praying with
Process Theology

SPIRITUAL PRACTICES FOR PERSONAL
AND PLANETARY HEALING

Bruce Epperly

PROCESS
CENTURY
PRESS

ANOKA, MINNESOTA 2022

Process Century Press
RiverHouse LLC
802 River Lane
Anoka, MN 55303

Cover: Susanna Mennicke

Process Century Press books are published in association with the International Process Network.

VOLUME I: FAITH IN PROCESS SERIES
JEANYNE B. SLETTOM, GENERAL EDITOR

ISBN: 978-1-940447-26-1
Printed in the United States of America

CONTENTS

A word of thanks

SECTION ONE: PROCESS THEOLOGY AND THE SPIRITUAL JOURNEY

1. Spirituality for a Pluralistic, Postmodern, and Planetary Age
2. Praying with Process

SECTION TWO: ADVENTURES OF THE SPIRIT

Week One: Loving God

Week Two.   Adventurous God

Week Three: Christ Is Alive

Week Four: Spiritual Adventures

Week Five: WorldTransforming Prayer

Week Six: Healing World

Week Seven: New Every Morning

A Final Word: The Adventure Continues

Selected Resources and Endnotes

Alfred North Whitehead's process philosophy develops and explores the concept that all existence is necessarily relational. Nothing is isolated: all things are interconnected. Such theories are now commonplace in many of the sciences, but they are also deeply resonant with religious and theological thought. Perhaps the most profound religious expression of process thinking is the necessarily interrelational nature of all things, not only to one another, but also and centrally to God. Internally and externally, we exist in and through relationships. Many forms of process theologies have been developed in the decades since relational thinking deepened our understanding of reality.

Process Century Press has published a number of works dealing with relational thought. But theoretical work has not been the only mode of working with the relational structure of all existence—to the contrary, many practical implications have also affected personal and communal forms of religion. In this Faith in Process series, the Press looks to contemporary resources that enhance religious life, both personally and communally. It may well be that there is no greater need for such works than our present time. Given the flux in the contemporary world—the merging of politics and faith, renewed questions about who "qualfiies" to lead religious activities, tensions between freedom and responsibility, the scope of freedom for women and their own bodies, issues of migration, continuing racism—there are issues enough! Relational forms of thinking are needed now more than ever. And because we are indeed relational, interwoven with one another at our deepest levels, it may even be possible that works exploring and promoting our relationships to one another and to God may be part and parcel of our healing.

Marjorie Hewitt Suchocki

A WORD OF THANKS

THIS BOOK IS A LABOR OF LOVE, emerging out of the Tenth Whitehead International Conference, "Seizing an Alternative: Toward an Ecological Civilization," June 4–7, 2015. The conference focused on the need for a new vision of reality to promote the healing of our planet. Earth is "in the balance," as former Vice President Al Gore claimed a decade ago. The time to seize the moment is now, for us and our children's children.

At the conference, I had the joy of leading a seven-session track focusing on "Frontiers of Process Theology." Although our focus was innovative images of process theology, our conversations turned toward the fate of the Earth We identifed the need for spiritual practices based on the insights of process theology to undergird our ecological commitments. These fifty days of devotional readings, grounded in the resources of process theology, were inspired by those conversations. I am grateful for my partners in our session: George Hermanson, Sheri Kling, Thomas Oord, Curtis Rigsby, and Martha Rowlett.

i

I am especially grateful to my theological mentors John Cobb, David Griffin, and Bernard Loomer and to creative colleagues and Claremont classmates from the 1970s: Jay McDaniel, Catherine Keller, Marc Ford, Sandra Lubarsky, Rita Nakashima Brock, and Rebecca Parker for our shared adventures in the transformation of process theology. I am grateful to Patricia Adams Farmer for reading and commenting on the text and to Jeanyne Slettom for her publishing and editing.

I am eternally grateful to my life companion Kate Epperly who encouraged me to attend the conference. After nearly forty years of marriage, I am discovering the missionary character of a healthy and loving marriage. The love we have for each other inspires us to seek healing for the world and for people marginalized by issues of sexual identity, economic status, race, and nation of origin. Our love also inspires us to care for the Earth and generations of human and nonhuman creatures we will never meet. I dedicate this book to my grandsons Jack and James, and all the other young children of the world, that they might have a world of beauty, wonder, justice, and love.

Process Theology and the Spiritual Journey

CHAPTER ONE

Spirituality for a Pluralistic, Postmodern, and Planetary Age

> The call forward is toward intensified life, heightened consciousness, expanded freedom, more sensitive love, but the way lies through the valley of the shadow of death. (John B. Cobb Jr., *God and the World*, 56)

Alfred north whitehead asserts that the recognition "all things flow" is essential to understanding our world and personal lives. The flow of life is a metaphysical principle describing the reality of the perpetual perishing that is characteristic of each moment of experience. Each moment of experience arises out of the universe and its immediate past in a lively process of creative transformation, then perishes in its immediacy, and lives on in its contribution to the ongoing evolution of the universe and the evolving memory of God.

The reality of change also describes our cultural and religious lives. Today, the religious landscape is in flux. The end of Christendom in North America is on the horizon; Christendom is already dead in Europe. The southern hemisphere is becoming the new center of gravity for a Pentecostal vision of the Christian faith.

Pluralism is on the rise, religiously and culturally. A growing number of persons describe themselves as "spiritual but not religious." Others see themselves as "none of the above" or "done" altogether with religious institutions due to boredom, irrelevance, trauma, or marginalization. Today, people have thousands of religious options just at the click of a mouse. A growing number of persons practice forms of "hybrid" spirituality or "inter-spirituality," joining the gifts of a variety of religious traditions to nurture their spiritual growth.

The ancient affirmation, "all things flow," is also descriptive of our ethnic, economic, and planetary context. North America is multicultural. The era of Euro-American ethnic domination is coming to an end, at least demographically. Nevertheless, in certain communities, racism is on the rise, reflected in church bombings, police violence against persons of color, and the use of the Confederate flag as a symbol of white supremacy. Calls to complete a wall between the United States and Mexico are on the rise, and politicians rail against undocumented workers and Muslim refugees from war-torn lands. Despite communications that create an aura of planetary unity, the gap between rich and poor is increasing, and the middle class is shrinking in North America. Planetary and spiritual unity is growing alongside religious violence and polarization.

Global climate change threatens the very survival of humanity. Drought, flood, and rising oceans put millions of persons at risk, jeopardize population centers, and create political instability. We are reaching a point in polluting our planet from which there may be no turning back. Our grandchildren's children may inherit a vastly different world than the one we were born into. Green space and days at the beach may become distant memories for the generations that succeed us. The beaches on Cape Cod, where I walk daily—and Cape Cod itself—may disappear in the next century as a result of rising ocean levels.

Over two thousand years ago, the early Christian teacher Paul of Tarsus counseled, "Do not be conformed to this world; but be transformed by the renewing of your minds, so that you can discern what is the will of God — what is good and acceptable and perfect." (Romans 12:2) The evidence is clear that we need a transformed personal and planetary consciousness. We need to move from individualism and consumerism to simplicity of life and a sense of the common good. We need to evolve in our personal lives and national allegiance from self-interest to world loyalty. We need a worldview that inspires transformed spiritual practices as well as personal and community commitments to justice and ecological healing. We need to align ourselves with God's vision of planetary healing.

I believe that process theology provides a practical, life-changing vision for our pluralistic, postmodern, and planetary age. If we take the process vision seriously, we will change our lifestyles and behaviors. We will join the personal and planetary to heal the world.

Our theological visions can cure or kill. Images of God emphasizing power, domination, and predestined privilege have led to planetary destruction and the eradication of indigenous people. Such visions have led theologian John Cobb to assert that, "The God of Christian theism is dying and deserves to die."[1]

In contrast to life-destroying theologies, we need theological visions that empower, heal, and inspire us to become God's companions in changing the world. Theology — and process theology, in particular — can be understood as a series of affirmations that can change our minds and change the world if held sincerely and practiced consistently. These affirmations are intimately connected with spiritual practices that enable us to experience the profound interconnectedness of life and our intimate companionship with a loving, living God. Grounded in the metaphysical visions of Alfred North Whitehead and Charles Hartshorne, process theology makes the following affirmations about the world in which we live.

Our world is a dynamic, ever-evolving process.
Relationship is primary to reality.

We live in a world characterized by dynamic interdependence.

We live in a universe of experience and this includes non-humans as well as humans.

Value is co-extensive with experience and reality.

Every creature has value and deserves ethical consideration, apart from human interests.

Creativity and freedom are essential to reality, including the nonhuman world.

The future is open and our actions make a difference in shaping the world to come.

Process theology presents an innovative global vision of God, consistent with the biblical witness that calls us to be God's companions in healing the Earth and its peoples. Process theology's vision of God undergirds our spiritual practices, ethical actions, and understanding of the power of prayer. While God cannot be fully encompassed by our theological visions, we can imagine God's nature in terms of the following affirmations:

God is present everywhere and in all things. (Revised version of divine omnipresence.)

God experiences everything and God's ongoing experience of the world is constantly growing in relationship to an evolving universe. (Revised version of divine omniscience.)

Although God influences all things, God's power is best understood in terms of love rather than coercion or domination. (Revised version of divine omnipotence.)

In all things, God works for good, even life's most challenging situations.

God's power is persuasive and invitational, a call forward, as the source of possibilities and ideals appropriate to every occasion of experience and our whole lifetimes.

The future is open for God as well as us.

God needs us to be partners in God's dream of world transformation.

In a dynamic, relational universe, permeated by God's creative wisdom, we make the following affirmations about our own spiritual journeys:

God is present in our lives as the "still small voice" (1 Kings 19:12) speaking in "our sighs too deep for words" (Romans 8:26).

Our spiritual practices bring God's unique and personal visions for our lives and the world to consciousness.

When we pray, we align ourselves with God's vision for us and experience greater divine energy.

Our prayers, in an interdependent universe, create a field of force that enables God to be more active in our lives and the lives of those for whom we pray.

Our prayers create new possibilities for divine and human activities and may influence the nonhuman world in amazing ways.

Living in the spirit of process theology provides a powerful inspiration for personal and global transformation. In the pages ahead, my goal is to present process theology in an accessible way and to provide spiritual practices that can be used by laypeople as well as religious and academic professionals. Process theology can change your life and change the world!

CHAPTER TWO

Praying with Process Theology

All creation is connected in God. God is a part of all creation. We meet each other in God. Our prayers for others and for the world make a difference in the interconnectedness of all reality. (Martha Rowlett, *Weaving Prayer in the Tapestry of Life*, 121)

RECENTLY, WHEN I TOLD my young grandchildren I had been meeting with my administrative assistant, one of them asked, "Were you meeting with your boss?" Although I have a collegial relationship with our church administrator and ministerial staff, I responded, "No, I'm the boss." My four-year-old responded, "No you're not. God and Jesus are the bosses." And, he was right! God and Jesus are the bosses of the church. Then he asked, "How do you know what God and Jesus want you to do?"

The answer to that question is at the heart of our spiritual journeys. God is constantly sharing visions with us. In every moment and encounter, God is giving us an array of possibilities and the energy to pursue them.

Grace is real, universal, and unconditional. God loves us and gives us life-transforming visions or possibilities regardless of our past behaviors. But often we forget God's constant care. We think we are alone in the world. We believe that authentic change is impossible both a personal and a global level. So are we doomed to lonely repetition? Are our futures sealed by past behaviors, divine will, or the impact of our family of origin? Or do we live in a God-inspired, open-ended universe, where change is possible for us and for our institutions? As one of my preaching mentors, Ernie Campbell, asserted, "There are only two kinds of people in the world. Those who are in God's hands and know it, and those who are in God's hands, and don't." Process theologians might amend this to include, "There are only two kinds of people in the world. Those who are inspired by God's call to creative transformation and know it, and those who are inspired by God's call to creative transformation, and don't know it." Spiritual practices help us recognize that we are in God's hands and that God has a life-transforming vision for us.

As a pastor and professor, I am committed to living process theology and making it come alive in my family, congregation, writing, and teaching. Process theology is a way of life, not just an intellectual game to play. I want to move from my armchair and laptop to the halls of Congress and daily decision-making, and to make process theology real in my life and in the lives of those to whom I pastor and relate. I want the vision of a lively, visionary, innovative, relational, loving, and freedom-loving God to come alive for them and shape their daily lives.

Process theology presents a prayerful and mystical vision of life in which God is always present, providing us with creative and life-supportive visions at every moment of life. The whole earth, as the prophet Isaiah discovered, is full of God's glory (Isaiah 6:1–8). Every creature praises God in its own way. As Jay McDaniel notes, "even the stars pray." We live in a God-filled universe, and can experience divine guidance and care every moment of the day. We may even become the answer to another person's prayer by our responses to God's guidance.

In process theology, we experience God in both the micro and the macro. Each moment of experience reveals divine possibilities and energy. In celebrating the Holy Here and Holy Now, we find peace of mind and ethical insight. Echoing Jesus' counsel to consider the lilies, Vietnamese Buddhist Thich Nhat Hanh monk says, "The miracle is not to walk on water. The miracle is to walk on the green earth, dwelling deeply in the present moment, and feeling truly alive."[2] God is found in truly experiencing this perpetually perishing moment. Seize the moment! The whole universe is revealed in every breath!

We experience peace and insight also in looking at the big picture of life. In seeing our lives as part of God's multi-billion year evolutionary adventure and our planetary journey, we gain a larger perspective on life in which our day-to-day stresses recede into the background. In committing ourselves to world loyalty and seeing our lives as contributing to healing the Earth and our community, our spirits expand and we follow the paths of mahatmas, bodhisattvas, and saints. We become Earth-healers rather than Earth-destroyers. In envisioning God's presence in the long haul of history, we receive the gift of perseverance that enables us to remain committed to global healing and transformation, despite the slow movement of the moral arc of history.

I believe that healthy spiritual formation involves the interplay of vision, promise, and practice. Our lives are guided by the vision of a relational universe and a lively relational and open-spirited God. We are inspired by the promise that we can experience the God we seek not just in the "pie in the sky by and by" but in the hardscrabble and glorious world of everyday life. We can commit ourselves to practices that make our relationship with God and the world come alive. We can become world healers, companioning with Jesus of Nazareth, the great sages of history, and our adventurously healing God.

In the pages that follow, you will be invited to "live" process theology. Each day begins with a quote from a process philosopher or theologian followed by a spiritual-devotional interpretation of that quote. From the quote and devotional passage emerge the following process spiritual practices: 1) spiritual affirmations, 2) actions that embody these affirmations, and 3) a process-oriented prayer. Over several weeks of living with process theology, you can move from an intellectual understanding of process theology to the experience of "living" process theology and acting it out in your daily life.

A brief note on language: Some of the quotations used herein are from books written before the shift away from exclusively male references to God. I have not attempted to rewrite these with gender-neutral language (although all the theologians quoted herein now use it). I encourage you to use pronouns for God that resonate best within you. Thus feel free to use the male pronouns you find in these pages, or substitute ones that open you more fully to God's presence.

Take your time with each day's text. You may choose to do the daily devotions one day at a time or you may decide to spend a few days praying with a particular devotion as your guide. Go at your own speed, letting each day's insights sink in and inspire you. You may study this text individually, with your family or a group of friends, or in a congregational study group.

You are embarking on a Holy Adventure of personal and planetary healing. The Fellow Sufferer and Joyful Companion is with you!

SECTION TWO

Adventures of the Spirit

WEEK ONE

Loving God

If the modern world is to find God, it must find him through love and not fear. (Alfred North Whitehead, *Religion in the Making*, 73)

ALFRED NORTH WHITEHEAD believed that the modern world must discover God as loving rather than as coercive. He noted the tragic choice of the Christian theological and ecclesiastical elite to follow the way of Caesar in preference to the humble Galilean Jesus. A god of power leads to behaviors that emphasize orthodoxy over community and uniformity over creativity. An omnipotent God who arbitrarily chooses certain people as beloved and others as outcasts leads to initiating crusades, destroying indigenous peoples, excommunicating persons holding minority viewpoints, and bombing office buildings and sacred spaces of those with whom we disagree. A dominating God who inspires dominion over the nonhuman world leads to making our world a garbage dump, as Pope Francis observed in his encyclical *Laudato Si'*.

Evangelical theologian Thomas Oord notes that love, not power, should be the primary defining characteristic of God's relationship to the world. According to Oord, "If love is the center of the biblical witness and the core of Christian experience, it should be the primary criterion for theology. Love should be the orienting concern and continual focus for speaking systematically about theology. We should discard ideas or theories that undermine love."[3]

In the spirit of the apostle Paul's letter to the Philippians, God's power is best understood in terms of relationship not separation (Philippians 2:5-11).God's love is creative; it brings forth beauty everywhere. God's love is also responsive, open to feeling the universe in its joy and sorrow. In contrast to Aristotle's "unmoved mover," untouched and uninterested in the world of change and imperfection, process theology affirms that God is the "most moved mover," embracing the totality of our experience. God is, according to Whitehead, the "fellow sufferer who understands." God influences us supremely, as Charles Hartshorne avers, "because he is supremely open to our influence."[4]

In the days ahead, we will experience the love of God and God's passion for healing and creative transformation through affirmations, prayers, transformative actions, and theological reflections. We will see incarnation as real and shaping our lives today. God is with us, seeking abundant life for all creation, human and nonhuman. God wants abundant life for every creature and feels the pain of the "least of these" — factory-farmed animals, refugee children, grieving parents, dying species, and persons facing incurable illness. God delights in our joy and wants all of us, including the nonhuman world, to experience the fullness of life, despite the realities of destruction and conflict.

God loves the world and God's love is empathetic. God experiences the tragic results of global climate change and wants us to change our ways. We no longer need to be "fruitful and multiply," as was necessary for our parents in the faith. God calls us to simplicity, stewardship, and sharing the Earth with all creation. Following God invites us to love the world God loves, practice simpler lifestyles, and claim our role as companions of creation, gardeners and healers of the world.

Day One
LOVING GOD

If the modern world is to find God, it must find him through love and not fear. (Alfred North Whitehead, *Religion in the Making,* 73)

When someone claims to be an atheist, I often reply, "Tell me about the God you don't believe in." After they describe their images of God, I typically respond, "If I thought God was like that, I'd be an atheist, too!"

Our images of God can cure or kill, welcome or isolate. Unhealthy images of God are a deterrent to belief for many people. They see believers claiming that God is an all-powerful ruler before whom we must bow or face the consequences. They are scandalized by their encounters with believers for whom religion is about hell-fire, brimstone, and facing judgment in this lifetime and the next. These ardent believers tell many seekers: "If you don't believe the right things, step out of line, or are gay, lesbian, or transgendered, your soul is in jeopardy." They also assert that, "terrorist acts, the AIDS pandemic, and hurricanes and earthquakes are God's punishment for our nation's sinful behaviors." Many followers of the all-powerful potentate disparage the evidence of global climate change, trusting consistently inaccurate prognostications of the Second Coming rather than obvious impact of human actions on our planet's resilient, yet delicate, ecology. Only God can destroy the Earth, these believers say, but in the meantime, let's use up its resources as profitably as possible!

When they view Christians holding these viewpoints, seekers rightly protest, "If this is what God is all about, then I want nothing to do with such a malevolent and amoral force."

Many of today's "nones," people who have left the church or are put off by their understandings of Christianity, believe that Christians and the God they worship oppose science, marriage equality, theological questioning, and ethnic and cultural diversity. You can fear such a god, and you may go to church to avoid damnation, but such a deity can never inspire authentic love. Such a god can only inspire the love of privilege and power, and hope for a payoff after God destroys the earth!

Process theology asserts unabashedly that God is love. Jesus once said, "I have come that they might have life, and have it abundantly" John 10:10). In a graduate seminar, nearly forty years ago, one of my mentors, process theologian David Griffin, described God's relationship with us this way: "God wants us to enjoy; God wants all of us to enjoy."

On one of our vehicles, we've placed the bumper sticker, "God loves the whole world, no exceptions." A loving God embraces all creation, human and nonhuman, and desires that each of us experience beauty, joy, and love. In contrast to a punitive God of guilt and shame-based religions, process theologians believe that when God looks at your life, God treasures your experience and imagines what you can become moment by moment. God wants you to flourish, to succeed, to grow spiritually and ethically. Even when we turn away from God, God provides possibilities that are "the best for that impasse."[5] We may give up on ourselves, but God never does. God loves the world, and God loves you and everyone in it.

Affirmative Spirituality

Throughout today, repeat the following affirmations to ground your experience of God's love for you and all creation. Affirmations open the door to new possibilities and a greater influx of divine energy. They enable us to transform our minds and transform our world.

God loves me and wants me to flourish.
God loves each creature and wants each one to flourish.

Active Spirituality

As you go through the day, take time to look deeply at everyone you meet, including the birds of the air and the lilies of the field. Look for the presence of the holy in a child, companion, spouse, or colleague. Imagine the holiness of birds, companion animals, wild animals, and the flora and fauna of life. In the spirit of the Hindu tradition, you may choose to greet each one with a silent affirmation such as *Namaste,* "the divine in me greets the divine in you." You may equally use the historic Christian blessing, "the Christ in me greets the Christ in you."

Praying with Process

Holy and loving God, your love embraces creation in its entirety. You love all creatures "great and small." Your creative wisdom gives life to all things. Awaken me to the beauty of all creation, human and nonhuman. Let me delight in your love for me and inspire me to share that love with everyone I meet. Let me be a creative companion in your quest to bring love and beauty to this world. Amen.

Day Two
DIVINE POETRY

God is the poet of the world, with tender patience leading it by his vision of truth, beauty, and goodness. (Alfred North Whitehead, *Process and Reality,* 346)

God is the ultimate poet and artist of creation. As Isaiah discovered in his encounter with God in the Jerusalem temple, the whole Earth is filled with God's glory. (Isaiah 6:1–8) Divine poetry is aimed always at truth, beauty, and goodness. God's aim is for us to experience wholeness and beauty—even tragic beauty—in all the seasons of life.

I experienced the poetry of God on a Cape Cod August morning, walking on Craigville Beach near my home. The day was bright and the wind gentle, the sea was shimmering like glass. An osprey mother was feeding her hungry chicks. On the horizon was the ferry to Nantucket, and a few sailboats, tacking in the sunrise breeze. I returned to witness the poetry of a marriage of nearly four decades over the breakfast table and give thanks for the artistry of ministry and teaching. As I finished my coffee, I rejoiced in the backyard symphony of singing birds and rustling branches. Surely, God is constantly inspiring us to be poets whose words and actions bring beauty to the Earth and its creatures.

The word "poetry" has its origins in the Greek *poesis,* to create or make. Divine poetry invites creaturely poetry. The imaginative Poet of the World invites us to be poets in our own realm. God is not jealous of our creativity. In fact, in an unfinished world, God wants—and needs—our creativity and companionship to add to the beauty of the world. You are a poet, even if your words are sheer prose. You can follow God's example and create in beauty, truth, and goodness wherever you are.

Imagine that! You are an artist of experience and a poet of relatedness. Imagine! God loves your creativity and the more creative you are, the more creative God can be in bringing beauty and wholeness to the world. Claim your vocation as God's creative companion in healing the earth.

Affirmative Spirituality

Today, out of the alphabet of your experience, what poetry can you bring forth? Take time to experience the fullness of divine poetry in your life by repeating the following theological affirmations through-out the day.

I experience divine poetry everywhere and in every encounter.

God wants me to be creative and poetic, to bring beauty to the world.

Active Spirituality

Whitehead asserts that the teleology of the universe is aimed at the production of beauty. Yet, humankind has often rendered the Earth ugly by razing forests and polluting streams, preferring consumption over appreciation, and putting nonhuman species and the human species in peril through actions that promote global climate change.

As poetic companions of the divine poet, today consider how you can contribute to the poetry of the Earth. This can be through something as simple as picking up litter on the beach or in your neighborhood, signing a petition to ban plastic bags in your municipality, using canvas bags for shopping, or becoming involved in local and global initiatives aimed at healing the Earth. Today, consider the places you are called to add beauty to the Earth and challenge humankind's destructive militarism and consumption.

Praying with Process

O Divine Poet, awaken us to beauty and invite us to be poets of the Spirit. Help us to see our lives as works of art and inspire us to claim your vision of truth, beauty, and goodness in every encounter and for the well-being of our planet. Amen.

Day Three
SAVING THE WORLD

The image—and it is but an image —the image under which this operative growth is best conceived, is that of a

tender care in which nothing is lost.... God saves the world
as it passes into the immediacy of his own life. It is the
judgment of a tenderness which loses nothing that can be
saved. It is also the judgment of a wisdom which uses what
in the temporal world is mere wreckage. (Alfred North
Whitehead, *Process and Reality*, 346)

Elizabeth Kübler-Ross once confessed, "I'm not ok and you're not ok,
but it's ok!" There is a lot of wreckage in our lives, mirrored in our
impact on the nonhuman world, flora and fauna, woodlands, and
streams. There is also a lot of interpersonal and political wreckage,
and it is evident in broken relationships, familial alienation, civil war,
and the widening gap between the wealthy and poor.

As Whitehead notes, life begins with a dream of youthful
idealism, innocence, and possibility, and culminates in the reality
of tragic beauty. In a world in which many of our images of God
are violent, abusive, and alienating, Whitehead asserts that the
energy of creation seeks wholeness. God is powerful, energetically
moving through billions of galaxies, creating and recreating. But,
more importantly for us, God grows our lives and the evolutionary
process with "a tender care in which nothing is lost." God saves the
world! God embraces our ambiguous adventures, treasures our best
intentions, and companions our failures, seeking to save what can
be saved and heal what is broken in us and the world.

Salvation, or wholeness, takes many forms. One of them is the
healing of memories and the transformation of the past in light of a
vision of future wholeness. This happens as a result of the interplay
of divine companionship and human responsiveness. God listens,
embraces, and transforms our lives. What we do truly matters to
God's experience now and forever. Our lives in their immediacy
perish, but live evermore in God's ongoing healing of the universe.

Our quests for justice, sometimes ambiguous and half-hearted,
are treasured by God. Our successes and failures are embraced by
God. Our fears and loves become part of God's quest to bring wholeness to the world. God knows us, and loves us, and uses our lives as

part of God's quest for truth, beauty, and goodness. Knowing God's healing presence in our lives, we are inspired to become God's healing partners bringing forth beauty from the wreckage of our lives and from the current planetary situation.

Affirmative Spirituality

Our lives matter to God. God accepts us fully and seeks our healing and wholeness even when we have made a mess of our lives and made the world into a trash heap. The sense that our lives truly matter to God inspires us to greater responsibility in caring for our planetary neighbors. These affirmations can transform your relationship with God:

My life matters to God.
God seeks to bring beauty out of my brokenness.

Active Spirituality

There is much tragedy and wreckage in our world and humankind is greatly responsible for planetary pain. The challenge of planetary healing is great and almost beyond our abilities. We are tempted to give up hope, become disheartened, and believe our lives make no difference to God and others. God wants and needs our imperfect lives, and God wants us to have a role in healing others and this good Earth.

To what situations are you called to respond in a healing manner? Whose life, in its "wreckage," are you called to support and heal with God's inspiration and grace? Pray for guidance in bringing healing to the world around you and to persons in all their ambiguity and pain.

Praying with Process

Holy God, there is much wreckage in our world and our lives. We confess our brokenness and the areas of our lives where we have harmed others and the Earth. Help us to claim our vocation as God's healing partners, bringing forth beauty and healing to every life and the world as a whole. Amen.

Day Four
LOVING POWER

> For a period I did not believe in God. Now I do. The God in whom I believe loves relentlessly. The God of love calls me and all creation to love in response. Love ultimately matters.... If love is the center of the biblical witness and the core of Christian experience, it should be the primary criterion for theology. Love should be the orienting concern and continual focus for speaking systematically about theology. We should discard ideas or theories that undermine love. (Thomas Oord, *The Nature of Love: A Theology*, xii, 2)

As a child growing up in the Baptist church, two of the first Bible verses I learned — along with "Jesus wept" — was "For God so loved the world that he gave his only begotten son so that whosoever believes in him shall not perish but have everlasting life" (John 3:16) and "God is love" (1 John 4:8). Love is the only characteristic clearly identified with God's nature.

Sadly, as theologian Thomas Oord notes, theologians and believers have often been more willing to sacrifice love to power or sovereignty in their understanding of God. They can't imagine sacrificial love, grounded in acceptance and not judgment, as the greatest power in the world. If God doesn't guarantee victory, winning every battle, what good is God? If God doesn't ensure that our side wins or that our enemies are defeated, how can we trust God?

Yet, when Jesus spoke of God as a parent, he redefined both parenting and divinity. As loving as we are, our parenting and grandparenting is partial, imperfect, and sometimes hurtful. Divine parenting is all-embracing, perfect, and healing. The power of love is the greatest power in the world because it never ends and has no boundaries in its care. It remains stalwart and supportive regardless of life's circumstances. In contrast a deity defined primarily by power is morally neutral. There is a certain ethical arbitrariness in doctrines such as predestination of the saved and unsaved or a divine love that cannot withstand our doubts and unbelief. Moreover, if God's love ends at the grave, then death is more powerful than God. We can cower before divine power, but not bow down in gratitude and love.

Love endures forever. Love embraces all things. Love even includes the nonhuman world, and may even embrace our nonhuman companions in the afterlife. When scripture says God loves the world, it doesn't give exceptions. God loves sharks and osprey. God cherishes the lilies of the field and the birds of the air. God treasures lakes and seashores, ponds and cranberry bogs, and embraces our enemies as well as our allies. As a wise teacher once stated, "God is a circle whose center is everywhere and whose circumference is nowhere." God's love encircles our lives and embraces our yesterdays, todays, and tomorrows to bring healing to us and the world.

Affirmative Spirituality

Given the tendency to exalt power over love in economics, politics, and theological reflection, we need constantly to affirm the centrality of divine and human love. We need to constantly remind ourselves that love alone brings the healing and wholeness we seek for ourselves and our world.

> God loves me and all creation.
> God's love embraces my enemies as well as my friends.

Active Spirituality

Today, simply take time to "choose love" in every situation. When you are tempted to judge or diminish others, you can make a choice to see them in light of God's love and treat them with a loving spirit. This doesn't mean accepting bad behavior or injustice—or behaviors that prize profits over people and consumption over sustainability. It means looking for a common humanity and trying to bring it out. It means challenging injustice in ways that aim at reconciliation and healing, recognizing our temptation to dehumanize our opponents or objectify those with whom we differ.

Praying with Process

Loving Wisdom, whose compassion and creativity embraces all creation, human and nonhuman, friend and enemy, give us large spirits and great hearts. Remind us that love endures forever and that when we love your creation, we bring healing to the world you love. Amen.

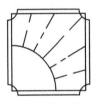

Day Five
DIVINE MIRRORING

> God is the ideal companion who transmutes what has been lost into a living fact within his own nature. He is the mirror that discloses to every creature its own greatness. (Alfred North Whitehead, *Religion in the Making*, 48)

God knows us fully, from the inside out. After describing his "perfect hatred" for those who oppose God's way, the Psalmist asks God to "Search me, O God, and know my heart; test me and know my thoughts. See if there is any wicked way in me, and lead me in the way everlasting." (Psalm 139:23–24) The Psalmist is sure of God's loving knowledge even when he falls into vindictiveness and alienation. In knowing he is known, the Psalmist finds healing and the ability to mend his ways.

All of us desire to be known and to have our whole selves accepted in their grandeur and pettiness. We share information with new friends or potential lovers in a pharmaceutical fashion, often beginning with our achievements and little by little sharing our imperfections and fears. In sharing intimacies, we are testing both ourselves and our new companions. We are trying to discern: How important is this relationship to me? Am I willing to be my whole self and trust that the other will accept me? Is there a point beyond which they will "flinch" and judge me as unworthy of their friendship or love?

God knows our lives completely in real time. As our lives unfold, they become part of God's life, not from the viewpoint of a disinterested observer but from that of a passionate and intimate companion.

Some knowledge is out to get us. Our imperfections are held against us, threatening our sense of worth and self-esteem. Our past mistakes hound us over the course of a lifetime. In contrast, process theology asserts that God's awareness is out to love us. God is completely on our side. The "ideal companion" knows us completely and loves us fully. God knows the impact of the past, our hidden fears, our most intimate dreams. God knows the challenges we face as we seek to live with integrity, balancing self-love with world loyalty. For God, our lives are a holy adventure, lived out in our day-to-day decisions.

In being known by God, we discover our own greatness. We glimpse the significance of our quotidian lives and the beauty of our day-to-day activities. God wants us to know that our finite and fallible actions are part of a bigger story—God's quest for beauty and wholeness in the evolution and transformation of our planet. In embracing God's awareness of our fallibilities, we experience our lives on a larger canvas. We discern the wisdom of the Jewish mystics, "when you save one soul, you save the whole universe," and awaken to the graceful greatness of our daily lives and our call to be God's companions in healing the world.

The times call for everyday people to experience their greatness and claim the great work of justice, mercy, and Earth care. Known and loved by God, we can risk failure, and in the process discover the amazing gift of sharing in God's quest for personal and planetary healing.

Affirmative Spirituality

God challenges us to grow in wisdom and stature, and to embrace as much reality as possible without losing our spiritual centers. Our quest is to become "little Christs" (Martin Luther) and Bodhisattvas, who transcend self-interest to embrace world-loyalty. This task of soul—making is moment by moment and day by day. It is sustained by a commitment to larger visions of ourselves and our impact on the world.

> God reveals to me my spiritual greatness and the importance
> of my actions in saving the world.
> God calls me to do something beautiful and great today.

Active Spirituality

God invites us to share in the great work of healing the world and our own lives and communities. The great work begins with simple steps and apparently insignificant, yet life-changing, actions. Be attentive throughout the day of opportunities to be part of God's great work. This work of creative transformation can be furthered by a kind word to a stranger, a phone call to congressional representative to support economic justice and planetary well-being, a morning devoted to cleaning up a local beach or public park, or participation in a congregational or community climate change awareness program.

Praying with Process

Insignificant though we seem and fallible though we are, O God, remind us of the significance of small actions in saving the world. Let our mustard seeds grow into trees of life that give shade to vulnerable persons or healing to the good Earth. Amen.

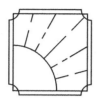

Day Six
GENTLE PROVIDENCE

The perfected actuality (in God) passes back into the temporal world.... the kingdom of heaven is with us today.... The action of the fourth phase is the love of God for the world. It is the particular providence for particular occasions. (Alfred North Whitehead, *Process and Reality*, 349)

"A particular providence for particular occasions," so writes the philosopher Whitehead in his description of God's presence in the world. Not just generic occasions of experience, moments of your life in general, but this particular moment is receiving guidance and energy from God. God inspires the emergence of each moment of our lives with a vision of possibility—indeed numerous possibilities—and the energy to fulfill God's dream in this time and place.

Each moment has a providential character, and, for those whose senses are open, each moment is heaven-sent, reflecting God's call and awaiting our creative response. God does not determine our lives or the world in advance. Despite the impact of the past, including God's presence in our lives, this holy moment is wide open, anticipating our own agency for ourselves and our local and global environment.

All moments have a missional quality. They lead us beyond self-interest to responsibility for life beyond this moment, our own future, and the future of those around us.

Providence is particular and unique, oriented to this moment and our time in history. Surely God's "call forward," to use John Cobb's description of God's influence in our lives, involves our pluralistic, postmodern, and planetary age in all its diversity and challenge. Our challenge is to seize this particular moment, incarnating God's providence, to join unity and diversity, tradition and novelty, and local and global. Toward what is God's providence guiding you and your community today? What possibility, embodied in your own creative process, will bring beauty and hope to the Earth? What action will contribute to the creation of a truly ecological civilization?

Affirmative Spirituality

Each moment is providential in nature. Spiritual practices such as the use of affirmations bring to consciousness the deepest impulses of divine wisdom for us and the world.

> *God's providence guides me in each moment.*
> *God's providence inspires me to bring wholeness to the world.*

Active Spirituality

A bench at Kirkridge Retreat Center counsels us to "picket and pray." Divine providence challenges us to action, and invites to take risks to bring greater wholeness and beauty to our relationships, community, and world. What one action can incarnate the "particular providence" of God that is luring you forward today? What action will lead to greater well-being for creatures outside your circle of relationships? Let your response draw you toward some world-healing and relational-healing activity.

Praying with Process

Holy Love, your providence is guiding me today. Moment by moment, help me to awaken to your guidance and take a risk to embody your vision for my life and the world today. Amen.

Day Seven
THE FELLOW SUFFERER
WHO UNDERSTANDS

God is the great companion—the fellow sufferer who understands. (Alfred North Whitehead, *Process and Reality,* 351)

As a child growing up in the Baptist church, I remember singing "What a friend we have in Jesus, all our sins and griefs to bear; what a privilege to carry everything to God in prayer." Love is receptive as well as active. Love responds as well as creates. To love is to be shaped by another's joy and sorrow. Process theology affirms, in the words of philosopher Charles Hartshorne, that God is the "most moved mover." Not aloof from our world, God feels our joy and sorrow from the inside. We are never alone, nor are we ever forgotten. More than that, God feels the joys and pain of the nonhuman world from the inside. God knows what it's like to soar like an eagle, to be a dog or cat curling up next to her or his human companion, or to mourn the loss of a life mate as do many birds and mammals.

God is the fellow sufferer who understands and the joyful celebrant who companions. Our feelings become God's feelings and then empathetically return to the world in understanding, mirroring, and the sharing of possibilities. God is love, and love cares. William Blake's "On Another's Sorrow" describes the interplay of divine and human love that nurtures and transforms.

> Can I see another's woe,
> And not be in sorrow too?
> Can I see another's grief,
> And not seek for kind relief?
>
> Can I see a falling tear,
> And not feel my sorrow's share?
> Can a father see his child

Weep, nor be with sorrow filled?

Can a mother sit and hear
An infant groan, an infant fear?
No, no! never can it be!
Never, never can it be!

And can He who smiles on all
Hear the wren with sorrows small,
Hear the small bird's grief and care,
Hear the woes that infants bear -

And not sit beside the nest,
Pouring pity in their breast,
And not sit the cradle near,
Weeping tear on infant's tear?

And not sit both night and day,
Wiping all our tears away?
O no! never can it be!
Never, never can it be!

He doth give His joy to all:
He becomes an infant small,
He becomes a man of woe,
He doth feel the sorrow too.

Think not thou canst sigh a sigh,
And thy Maker is not by:
Think not thou canst weep a tear,
And thy Maker is not near.

O He gives to us His joy,
That our grief He may destroy:
Till our grief is fled and gone
He doth sit by us and moan.

Affirmative Spirituality

God's love inspires our love. Affirmative spirituality takes us beyond narrow and parochial loves to embrace the joy and sorrow of all creation in companionship with the fellow sufferer who understands.

> *God shares my joy and sorrow.*
> *Loved fully by God, I embrace creation lovingly.*

Active Spirituality

God is a verb, and so is love. Concrete and empathetic, love is the greatest power. Love is a divine force that seeks wholeness for all creation. Let your spiritual life guide you to listen more empathetically and imaginatively to the feelings of others, including the nonhuman world. Pause and truly listen, letting go of your inner dialogue and judgments, to a child, a vulnerable elder, your life companion, or a friend. Pause and listen to the birds waking the world this morning or experience the contentment of a companion animal lying beside you. Imaginatively feel the pain of creation, victimized by human carelessness and greed. Perhaps read Dr. Suess's *Horton Hears a Who,* and consider its theme, "a person's a person no matter how small." What is it like to be part of a living universe, filled with experiencing creatures (panexperientialism)? What actions will you take now that you affirm the universality of joy and sorrow, and God's commitment to treasure the experiences of nonhumans as well as humans?

Praying with Process

Help me listen to the cries of creation. Help me breathe with all creation, empathetically experiencing the joy and pain of this good Earth. Let me experience life as God does, celebrating and mourning, and let me empathy find embodiment in words and acts of love. Amen.

WEEK TWO

The Adventurous God

God entertains a purpose for the new occasion, differing from that entertained by the previous human experience. He seeks to lure the new occasion beyond the mere repetition of past purposes and past feelings or new combinations among them. God is thus at once the source of novelty and the lure to finer and richer actualizations embodying that novelty. Thus God is the One who calls us beyond all that we have become to what we might be. (John B. Cobb Jr., *God and the World*, 82)

ALFRED NORTH WHITEHEAD speaks of worship as an adventure of the Spirit. Faithful in all of life's changes, God's mercies are new every morning. God seeks to go beyond old orthodoxies and the idols of yesterday toward a vision of Shalom. God's call, as John Cobb asserts, moves us forward to new possibilities. There is always more light to be shed on the scripture and more wisdom to be found in creation. As the United Church of Christ affirms, "God is still speaking."

God is always doing a new thing. God's vision evolves the galaxies and planets, inspires the moral arc of history, and now guides us toward new horizons of liberation and Earth-care. God's adventurous love liberates peoples today and invites us to expand our moral concern to embrace the non-human world. The pathway of discipleship opens us to new dimensions of mission and planetary consciousness. Wherever we go on our own adventures, a fellow adventurer will be our companion.

Day One
INCARNATING GOD

> Every event on its finer side introduces God into the world. . . . the power by which God sustains the world is the power of himself as the ideal. . . . The world lives by the incarnation of God in itself. (Alfred North Whitehead, *Religion in the Making*, 149)

I begin each day with the affirmation, "This is the day that God has made, I will rejoice and be glad in it" (Psalm 118:24). Process theology goes even further with the affirmation, "This is the moment God has made, I will rejoice and be glad in it." God is present in every moment of life as the source of vision and possibility and as the energy incarnate in the truth, beauty, and goodness in our lives. How different this is from beginning the day with a sense of hopelessness and dread.

God is in all things, and all things are in God. God is present in the part, this arising moment of experience, and also in the whole, in the coordination of possibilities for our lives, our communities, and the planet. Our vocation is to discern God's ideals for our lives moment by moment and over the long haul and then embody them in our thoughts and actions.

God is here, within, as the still small voice, moving creatively in all things. This is the image of God, inherent in humankind, and the source of the holiness of each life. This is also the source of the value of the nonhuman world, apart from human interests. God is incarnate in the experiences of osprey, sharks, monarch butterflies, chimpanzees, and hummingbirds. God delights in the flight of the eagle, the imagination of a young child at play, and an artist painting a seascape. Divine presence in creation grounds our reverence in life and our commitment to support life in all its variety. It brings beauty and wonder to every encounter.

Affirmative Spirituality

Believing is seeing. Affirmations awaken us to God's presence in our lives and in the nonhuman world.

> *My life incarnates God's wisdom.*
> *The nonhuman world incarnates divine wisdom.*

Active Spirituality

The incarnation of God in every event inspires reverence for life. While no creature or moment of life is absolute, each life should be treasured. Today, look deeply at those around you. Can you experience wonder and beauty for those with whom you live and love? Can you see holiness in companions at the coffee house or drivers on the freeway? Can you practice reverence for life when you consider politicians who "push all your buttons" with their rhetoric and reactionary assertions? Can you see the divine in the world of spotted owls, lizards, spiders, and ocelots? Do you, like Jesus, see glory in the wild grasses and birds of the air? Discover ways you can cultivate a holy vision and then move from reverence to healing actions.

Praying with Process

Incarnate in me, O Divine Wisdom, your love and wisdom. Help me honor the holiness of my life and the holiness of all creation. Amen.

Day Two

THE BEST FOR THE IMPASSE

> The initial aim is the best for that impasse. (Alfred North Whitehead, *Process and Reality*, 244)

An impasse, by definition, is a reality that we must eventually face. The Merriam-Webster dictionary defines it as "a predicament affording no obvious escape" or a "cul-de-sac." The one reality we can't avoid is the process of self-creation, emerging from a settled past, environmental context, and our own previous decisions. We must face the world as it is to create the world as it should be.

God doesn't punish us for the past. Still, although God constantly seeks abundant life for us and all creation, God must adapt to the world as it is. Our actions and the environment around us can limit or enhance God's presence in the world and our lives. The concrete world created by our decisions and the decisions of others is the womb of possibility for us and for God. Our ethical and spiritual challenge is to create a world, one decision at a time, that promotes the most creative, inspirational, and energetic possibilities.

Spiritual formation involves moment-by-moment attentiveness to God's initial aim or ideal for any given situation. In bringing God's vision to awareness, we open the door to a greater impact of divine possibility for each succeeding moment of experience.

The best for the impasse may be "bad," Whitehead notes. In our current context, the quest for an ecological civilization will be painful. It must involve sacrifice and turning away from habits of consumption, profit-making, and independence. We may have to jettison certain sought-after possibilities to promote a sustainable future. Yet, living simply so others can simply live opens us to an array of new possibilities, luring us to positive relationships with our human and nonhuman companions.

Spiritual Affirmations

"God is still speaking" is an affirmation used by the United Church of Christ to describe God's ongoing revelation to humankind. A rejoinder to this affirmation is "But are we listening?" Affirmations create a space for listening to divine possibilities.

> *Each moment brings new possibilities to heal the world.*
> *My openness to God paves the way for a sustainable future.*

Active Spirituality

Jewish mysticism asserts that when you save one soul, you save the world. Conversely, the destruction of one soul damages the fabric of creation. Each moment can tip the world toward life or death, and we are part of that process. Practicing spiritual mindfulness—awareness of our deepest "heart's desire"—opens us to intuit and live by God's world-healing possibilities. Devote one action at a time to bringing God's vision of truth, vision, and goodness to the world. The future is created in the synergy of humanity and divinity one moment at a time.

Praying with Process

In a world of conflict, O God, give us a larger perspective on our lives. Embedded in the moment, help us to embrace the future and act to insure the futures of generations to come. Let us bring peace and healing to this good Earth. Amen.

Day Three
RISKING ADVENTURE

The lure is not like a memo dictating to us the best course of action. We are called to improvise. We are called to

risk the adventure. For our adventure is inseparable from
the divine creativity: the unfolding of the world is not a
preprogrammed drama. How dreary would it be for God to
predict it all. But neither are we quite on our own with these
choices, these risks. (Catherine Keller, *On the Mystery,* 100)

I often remind my congregants that "while I always have a vision,
I seldom have an agenda." A vision is open-ended, slightly vague,
and content with a variety of outcomes. An agenda is specific and
is judged as a failure if our results fall short of our expectations or if
we have to take any detours along the way.

I believe God has a vision for both the moment and the long
haul, for individuals and communities, but no absolute writ-in-stone
agenda. God is the ultimate visionary and improviser. Like a jazz
musician, God's vision has many possible trajectories, each of which
leads to even more possibilities. God invites us to improvise as well.
Improvisation means risk, but it also means adventure. Historically,
adventurers, whether European or Asian, seldom arrived at their
desired destination. Instead, they discovered lands beyond their
imagination. J.R.R. Tolkien affirms that "all who wander are not
lost" and an adventurous God is also a wandering God, guiding the
hardscrabble Hebrew people across the wilderness, meandering and
yet moving toward a promised future. God is guiding us, despite our
own starts and stops, toward a global, ecological civilization.

Adventures often appear to fail in their quests. But, like scien-
tific experimentation, failure is part of the learning process. This
applies to God as well as to us. Just think about all the "failures" in
our planet's evolution. Where have all the dinosaurs gone? Where's
that gigantic shark megalodon? Yet apart from the demise of the
dinosaurs, some suggest as the result of a meteor strike, humankind
would have never evolved.

Today, we have divine abilities to shape the future of our planet for
good or for ill. The adventures we have taken in science, technology,
and discovery are monumental. Yet, our technological advances are
bringing us closer to oblivion. Global climate change portends the

death knell of one adventurous trajectory and inspires to chart new adventures of creativity, congruent with planetary flourishing.

God has not given us a memo, entitled "How to Save the Planet," but God has presented us with an array of possible pathways, all risky, and all demanding change. Yet to continue following the now untenable pathways of consumption and destruction will eventuate in the demise of humankind and many of its creaturely companions.

A new planetary adventure calls, with multiple pathways and variations. The adventure ahead is holy in its synergies of spirit and flesh, values and technology, and in its willingness to pursue "downward mobility" in the developed countries to ensure an upward course of earthly life for all our planetary companions.

We aren't on our own; we have God as our companion and guide. Succeed, fail, or arrive at an unexpected destination, our quest for planetary healing will always be treasured by the Fellow Sufferer and Adventurous Companion who understands and inspires.

Affirmative Spirituality

Adventure requires inspiration. Often we need to follow the example of *The Little Engine that Could* and repeat "I think I can, I think I can" to bolster our courage and creativity as we face challenges beyond our perceived abilities.

> God invites me to improvise and create.
> God is my companion on every adventure.

Active Spirituality

Every adventure begins with a dream, followed up by small, almost infinitesimal, first steps. Sometimes we take the step on the inside first and then let it emerge in a new behavior or the journey to a new land. Transformation can occur at any time, often with little or no warning. We can go beyond perceived limitations to discover new possibilities for ourselves and the planet. Once upon a time, writing a book seemed like something beyond my abilities. Now, nearly twenty-five years after my first book, I've published over forty books. Five loaves and two fish can barely feed a growing boy. Yet, the boy steps forward, and a multitude is fed.

What adventure lures you forward? What life-transforming possibility haunts your dreams? Let that dream soak in. Perhaps it involves pursuing a new talent or pushing beyond previous limitations. It may involve a changed behavior to promote better health. Or, it may be planetary in dimension, inspiring you to challenge an environmental hazard in your neighborhood or take the first step in preserving a local beauty spot or species.

Praying with Process

Help us, O Adventurous God, to dream big and follow our dreams to new horizons of hope. Amen.

Day Four
ON EARTH AS IT IS IN HEAVEN

> The desire to live more abundantly is part of God's prayer within each human heart. At its most basic level, it is a desire for happiness, for ourselves and ultimately for all living beings. This desire belongs to both God and us. Not only are we co-creators with God, we are co-desirers, co-prayers. No less than God, our deepest prayer is that the will of God be done "on earth as it is in heaven." (Jay McDaniel, *Living from the Center,* 74)

The apostle Paul describes God's Spirit praying within us in sighs too deep for words. We don't always know what we need, but God provides wisdom congruent with our life situation and personal and communal context. The apostle Paul also asserts that our deepest longings are part of creation's cries for wholeness. Creation has been wounded by human sin, and, like ourselves, the nonhuman world needs God's healing touch, embodied in personal and global transformation.

Spiritual practices help us identify God's prayer within our prayers and then live in synch with God's vision for us, humankind, and the planet. God wants us to live more abundantly, and this divine desire applies to all creation. While "life is robbery," [5] that is, our survival requires the sacrifices of other creatures, nonhuman as well as human, we need to ponder the questions: "How do best seek abundant life for others, including nonhumans, as well as ourselves? What does it mean for relatively affluent persons in developed countries to seek abundance in the context of a global village in which many people, even in developed countries, barely have the resources to survive from day to day? What does our abundance mean and toward what should we aspire when our thirst for fossil fuels threatens polar ice caps, life at the poles, Amazon rain forests, and the entire planetary ecosystem?"

We need to listen deeply to the cries of creation within our own aspirations and anxieties. In an interdependent universe, we can hear and respond to the pain of the nonhuman as well as human world. How will our awareness of the cries of creation transform our attitudes and behaviors so that we move from self-interest to world loyalty?

Affirmative Spirituality

Process affirmations open us to hear the cries of creation and the pain of our fellow humans. In listening deeply, we discover that our prayers take us beyond our interests to love creation with the same care that we love ourselves and our families.

God's spirit speaks to me through my prayers.
In prayer I hear the cries of creation and respond with loving care.

Active Spirituality

When we are aligned with God's vision, our prayers can be factors in transforming the world. As biblical scholar and spiritual guide Walter Wink noted, the future belongs to the intercessors. Listen deeply to your prayers today. Listen for other voices in your voice. Ask God to direct you to a particular need in your community (addiction, childhood poverty, homelessness, pollution, animal welfare, poverty among the elderly). We need to care for both the human and nonhuman communities to heal the world. What one new thing can you do to bring to your world, local and global? Where do you need to focus your prayer life today?

Praying with Process

We thank you, Divine Adventurer, for the wonders of life, the intricacy of our bodies and the grace that fills the nonhuman world. Too often we have been senseless and apathetic, ignoring the beauty around us and the desperate cries of creation. Awaken us to wonder and to actions that heal this good Earth. Amen.

Day Five
LIVING WORDS

> The meaning of a text is open-ended evolving with the creative advance of the world. (Ronald Farmer, *Beyond the Impasse*, 83)

God is constantly doing a new thing. As the author of Lamentations proclaims, "God's mercies never come to an end: they are new every morning. Great is God's faithfulness." (Lamentations 3:22–23) Fidelity is revealed in change and transformation, in revealing new possibilities for a new era. In contrast, many people freeze revelation in some past era. They see revelation and scripture as unalterable, unrelated to historical change. They affirm "God said it, I believe it, and that settles it," as if to say that God is also frozen in time and unrelated to historical change and human evolution. I believe that a living God is also a changing God. God's vision of truth, beauty, and goodness is sure and certain, but the manifestations of divine wisdom vary according to time and place.

Scripture is the beginning and not the end of our quest to know God. In the spirit of the rabbis, scripture gives birth to novel forms of Midrash and interpretation over time. There is always more light and wisdom to be found in our understanding of scripture and revelation because the Inspirer of scripture is always on the move. God is doing a new thing. God is faithful, and God's mercies are new every morning.

Revelation, whether biblical or personal, requires receivers who change the shape and meaning of it over time. Passages on slavery, marriage, or homosexuality need to be understood in their historical setting and also reinterpreted to respond to our current situation. If the teleology of the universe is aimed at beauty, then our quest to bring greater beauty to the world challenges texts that encourage oppression and marginalization.

Our God is living and loving and constantly creating in response to our creativity and the challenges of our time. God is speaking to us today in whispers, social activism, and the growing concern for Earth care. Let us listen and respond to take place as voices in God's continuing revelation to humankind.

Affirmative Spirituality

Living faith is open to new expressions and new voices. Today's cultural, spiritual, and planetary situation invites us to listen to the voices of marginalized peoples, persons of other faiths, and our nonhuman companions.

God is revealing wisdom in my life.
I am open to new and varied voices of divine wisdom and
*   revelation.*

Active Spirituality

If you belong to a religious community, you may choose to sponsor a conversation on revelation, scripture, and faith. Scripture is at the heart of the Christian faith tradition. Accordingly, we need to reflect on the nature of scriptural authority and its role, positive and negative, in responding to our current religious and planetary climate. What sources of revelation are important to us? How shall we understand the "difficult" passages of scripture? In what ways can we creatively appropriate the wisdom of other religious traditions? How might a different approach to scripture change our values and actions?

Praying with Process

Living God, your mercies are new every morning, and your wisdom emerges with each new day. Help us to listen to new revelations, coming from unexpected places and persons. Help us to read scripture as a living document, whose meaning speaks to the present as well as the past. Help us to hear you in the cries of nature and in our own inner spiritual hungers. Help us open to the wisdom of persons of other faiths and the insights of forgotten peoples. Help us grow in faith as we experience your grace in all creation. Thank you, God. Amen.

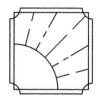

Day Six
WEAVING A LIFE OF GRACE

> You can blame God for this horrible curse, making God into some kind of monster who does wicked things such as this [multiple sclerosis]. Or you could let go of those worn out images of the Divine and help God weave something novel of your life as it is. For God is the gentle weaver who works with each ill-matched thread to bring about novel patterns of meaning and hope. (Patricia Adams Farmer, *Embracing a Beautiful God,* 55)

In nearly forty years of pastoral and academic ministry, numerous people have come to my study trying to fathom their personal experiences of "the problem of evil." Most are initially quite confused. Others are angry at God or ashamed of behaviors that they believe have led to the pain their experiencing.

Many are troubled by pastoral counsel they have received, such as "Your cancer is God's will. You simply have to accept it"; "God is testing you, trying to strengthen your faith"; or "God is punishing you for your teenage promiscuity." Still others believe that we are solely responsible for our suffering. New age pundits blithely proclaim, "You create your own reality. Your negativity brought that illness into your life." Similar to the new age pundits whom they denounce as godless, some proponents of the "prosperity gospel" assert that "if you only have enough faith, you'll get well. You're sick because of sin and faithlessness. If you take a chance on God, and contribute to our ministry, good things will come into your life. You will get the salary and job you want."

Process theology takes a very different path. It affirms our freedom and creativity to bring healing into our lives. Healthy theology proclaims some important truths about God's relationship to us:

- God seeks abundant life and healing for us.

- God's power is loving and not coercive.

- God is not responsible for suffering and evil; God's aim is to comfort those who suffer and provide possibilities for wholeness and healing.

- God is working for good in all things, including our negative past. God uses the wreckage of our lives to bring healing to us and the world.

It has been said that spirituality involves the "unfixable" aspects of life, including the inevitable realities of aging, sickness, and death. Encountering the Gentle Weaver in our weakness, we discover that God is on our side and that God's grace is always sufficient for us, even in our most difficult moments.

Affirmative Spirituality

As Gautama the Buddha discovered, pain is inevitable. Suffering comes when we hold onto the way things were, or our hopes for a pain-free existence, rather than discovering that all things must pass, and that peace comes from accepting the reality of impermanence. Perception shapes our experiences, bringing joy or sorrow and shaping our responses to situations beyond our creation or control. Affirmations invite us to experience our lives in ways that promote well-being and peace of mind.

> God is the gentle weaver who seeks wholeness in all things.
> God is giving me courage and imagination to face with boldness
> and creativity what is beyond my control.

Active Spirituality

God's gentle providence offers certain persons in our lives to be companions in a healing adventure. Sometimes we are the ones in need of support and counsel. Other times, our calling is to share a healthy vision of God as we mirror others' pain and sorrow. Prayerfully ask God to sensitize you to the pain in your midst and awaken you to persons in need of your care. When someone in need of healing comes into your life, take time to pause and notice God's vision for this relationship and then open to God's creative-responsive love. Let your goal be to become a healing partner, whose spiritual attentiveness opens the door for healing possibilities for one in need of your care.

Praying with Process

Awaken us, Gentle Weaver, to your vision of healing for myself, others, and the world. Open my heart to deeper love and my mind to greater possibilities. Help me share in your healing power and love one person at a time. Amen.

Day Seven
FAITH AND DOUBT

> Because I believe in God, I find it supremely important to reconsider and doubt my belief. And because God is of ultimate importance, how we think of God deeply affects how we live. Every misunderstanding of God reflects itself in a misdirection of human energy. (John B. Cobb Jr., *Can Christ be Good News Again?* 36)

Theologian Paul Tillich once averred that doubt is an essential aspect of faith. Doubt is the other side of belief. God and the evolving universe are greater and more mysterious than we can imagine. A universe of over 125 billion galaxies, each of which has billions of suns like our own, can never fully be fathomed. The horizon of knowledge is receding even as we venture toward it.

Our viewpoints, even those we are willing to live and die by, are always finite, partial, and perspectival. We can catch a glimpse of the Holy One, but never the whole reality. As Christians, we believe that Jesus of Nazareth, the Christ, reveals God's character as loving, relational, affirming, and embracing of diversity. This is enough for us to live gracefully from day to day, and to die with confidence in God's all-embracing love. Yet the many manifestations of divine wisdom, in other cultures and religious traditions and perhaps in other solar systems and galaxies, serve to challenge any attempt to limit God's love or creativity. It also inspires adventures of the Spirit in which we open ourselves to other visions of God and the ultimate realities, emerging from the interplay of God and human experience. God has many sides and approaches us in many ways. Joyful and grateful doubt testifies to our trust that the God who is always more never tires of providing possibilities for wholeness appropriate to our situation and the situations of every creature.

Radical amazement and awe, according to Jewish theologian Abraham Joshua Heschel, are appropriate responses to our wondrous Companion, whose creative wisdom is always more than we can ask or imagine. In light of the glories of creation and its Creator, let us embrace our finitude and doubt and trust that God will provide enough guidance for our personal healing and the healing of the planet.

Affirmative Spirituality

Affirmations are lenses through which we experience reality. They are never final or complete as they open us to images of personal and planetary transformation.

> I rejoice in the grandeur of God and God's many revelations
>   in human and non-human experience.
> In my finitude and imperfection, I trust the grace of God.

Active Spirituality

According to my dear friend and colleague, Rabbi Harold White, Jewish theologian Martin Buber asserted that "reality is not always understandable but it is embraceable." We can never fully fathom the mystery of God or another person. This can lead to misunderstanding; it can also lead to humility and appreciation and the recognition that the realities we encounter can be described and approached in many ways. This is especially important in our postmodern, pluralistic world. We may not always understand another person's faith, but we can seek to be empathetic and learn from their images of the divine.

This appreciative humility is an antidote to the polarization characteristic of our political and religious worlds. Humility that is grounded in recognition of the limitations of our most deeply held beliefs enables us to grow spiritually and intellectually and to discern the insights hidden in belief systems with which we disagree. Such empathetic openness is our only hope for finding common ground in our quest for a just and ecological civilization.

Throughout the day, listen to others' deeply held beliefs. Hear the truths hidden in their "falsehood" as you look for common ground. When you disagree, creatively challenge their beliefs without diminishing or judging them as persons. Do not succumb to the hate speech and derision characteristic of much social media communication. Speak your truth with love and respect, and encourage continuing dialogue.

Praying with Process

God of galaxies and spinning solar systems, awaken us to radical amazement. Help us to experience your wisdom in the micro world and the macro world and grow in reverence for life in all its manifestations. Amen.

WEEK THREE

Christ Is Alive

God entertains a purpose for the new occasion, differing from that entertained by the previous human experience. He seeks to lure the new occasion beyond the mere repetition of past purposes and past feelings or new combinations among them. God is thus at once the source of novelty and the lure to finer and richer actualizations embodying that novelty. Thus God is the One who calls us beyond all that we have become to what might be. (John B. Cobb Jr., *Can Christ be Good News Again?* 36)

TODAY MANY SEEKERS LOVE JESUS but hate Christianity. They identify Jesus with acceptance, healing, loving hospitality, healing, and care for the least of these. In contrast, they view Christianity as intolerant, anti-science, inhospitable to strangers and immigrants, small-minded, and antagonistic to gays and lesbians.

Process theology sees Christ as alive, transforming persons and communities. Jesus challenges the old order in light of God's vision of Shalom. As a child of the prophets, Jesus presents us with an alternative vision to consumerism, racism, intolerance, and speciesism. Jesus heals persons and institutions and invites us to ever-expanding circles of loving-kindness.

Jesus loved the least of these, both human and nonhuman. He embraced the marginalized, whether they were hated Samaritans, women of ill repute, agents of the oppressor, or persons with illnesses that rendered them socially unacceptable. Jesus treasured children, lilies of the field, and birds of the air. His healing touch transformed cells as well as souls.

John Cobb asks, "Can Christ be good news?" and invites us to embrace Christ-like behaviors that embrace diversity in all its forms. Whether they are Christians, seekers, or persons of other faiths, all persons can incarnate the "mind of Christ," seeing creation with the loving eyes of Jesus.

Christ is alive! Christ's spirit can creatively transform us and give us the vision and energy to transform our world. That is our calling as followers of the Healer from Nazareth.

Day One
GOD IS WITH US

> The One who is met in Jesus is the God who suffers with us and for us more than the God who demands and judges from on high. (John B. Cobb Jr., *God and the World,* 37)

Christian process theology is profoundly theocentric. It is also deeply Christ-centered and sees the life of Jesus as revealing the heart of God and the depth of God's love for the world. Sadly, many Christians have separated God and Jesus in terms of character and intent: God is a distant and demanding father, while Jesus is a loving friend. In contrast, process theology follows Jesus' own affirmation that "I and the father are one." If you want to know God, look to Jesus' forgiveness of those who persecuted him, his welcome of outcasts and marginalized people, his challenge to the religious and cultural status quo, and his commitment to healing and wholeness.

Jesus is "Emmanuel," God-with-us, experiencing our lives in all their wonder, beauty, pain, and ambiguity. Jesus asserted that "as you have done unto the least of these, my brothers and sisters, you have done unto me" (Matthew 25:40). This is not just an ethical admonition; it is a metaphysical one as well. Our actions matter to God. What we do shapes God's experience and brings greater or lesser beauty into the world and into God's experience.

Jesus' prophetic words challenge us to personal and global transformation. These challenges, however, come from within our world—from One who embraces our lives—and not a distant, unfeeling potentate. Jesus inspires us today precisely because he reveals who God is and who we are. As an early church theologian proclaims, "the glory of God is a person fully alive." Jesus is fully alive and shows us the pathway to abundant life, to human life at its fullest. Thanks be to God, the Parent of Jesus Christ, our inspiring guide and fellow sufferer who understands!

Affirmative Spirituality

Jesus is God's "yes" to the world. Jesus' ministry invites us to say "yes" to our becoming God's healing partners, committed to the well-being of humankind and the non-human world.

> *God is with me in every situation.*
> *I look to Jesus as my spiritual and moral guide in every*
> *situation.*

Active Spirituality

"The glory of God is a fully alive person." God invites us to become fully alive and to help others achieve their full humanity. Yet social structures, economic systems, and ecological destruction are often impediments to persons achieving their full potential. Take time to explore social and economic practices in your community and the larger world that stunt human possibility and pray for discernment in responding. Consider becoming a member of a group that sees human and nonhuman well-being as a social, economic, and ecological issue. (Many such groups abound, for example, Pando Populous, Bread for the World, International Fund for Animal Welfare, Creation Care, New England Regional Environmental Movement, and the Sierra Club.)

Praying with Process

Loving God, your companionship and care are amazing. You know our joys and pain and guide us toward abundant life. You show us what it means to be fully human and guide us to care for your children everywhere. Help us to know that our lives are our gifts to you, and that as we bring beauty to the lives of others, we bring beauty to your life as well. Amen.

 *Day Two*
CHRIST WITHIN ME

Christ is the giver of life to all who live, of freedom to all who are free, of understanding to all who understand, of love to all who love. Apart from Christ, there could be no life, no reason, no imagination, no personal or social redemption. But neither in Jesus, nor elsewhere, does Christ compel human beings to respond to the divine gift, promise, and call. Christ does not act as one agent alongside others, but in the empowering and directing of every agent. (John B. Cobb Jr., *Can Christ be Good News Again?* 36)

Christ is in us, the hope of creative transformation and a glorious future. Christ is also present in the world as a whole. John's Gospel asserts that "the true light enlightening all persons was coming into the world" (John 1:1–9). The Gospel of Thomas proclaims, "Cleave the wood and I am there" (Saying 77). God empowers and directs every creature persuasively, at the deepest levels of experience. When we say "yes" to divine creativity, we become God's partners in healing the world. This is surely good news for all creation.

Christ's work, however, is not merely related to individualistic spirituality. Our warmed hearts, as John Wesley said, lead to "practical divinity," to embodying God's grace in all of our behaviors. As John Cobb writes, "apart from Christ...there could be no personal or social redemption."

Let us, as the early Christian teacher Paul counseled, have the "mind of Christ," loving, extravagant in welcome, open to novelty, related to the great and the humble, and willing to sacrifice, so that God's realm of Shalom can take birth in our midst.

Affirmative Spirituality

Affirmations open us to the mind of Christ, the vision of holiness, and reverence for all creation.

> *I experience the world and every person through the mind of*
> *Christ.*
> *Christ beckons me to be a healing partner in every situation,*
> *personal and political.*

Active Spirituality

Aligning with the mind of Christ shapes our personal and social commitments. In many Benedictine monasteries, you will see a plaque reminding you to "Greet Everyone as Christ." Make a commitment to see everyone through the "eyes of Christ" and make every decision, shaped by the "mind of Christ." You might, in the spirit of the Social Gospel text, *In His Steps,* by Charles Sheldon, ask yourself at any point of decision, "What would Jesus do?" Then, listen to the voice of God within your experience and act on it with grace and love.

Praying with Process

Loving Jesus, your cup of love fills me with living waters. Your blessed bread fills me with abundant life and gives me strength for the journey. Open my senses to experience the world through your senses and greet the world with your love. Amen.

Day Three
FINDING CHRIST IN
UNEXPECTED PLACES

In Jesus we find incarnate not only the creative, directive, and redemptive activity of God, but God's suffering love as well. "Christ" names all this. It is for this reason it is profoundly true that what we do to the poor and the oppressed, we do also to Christ—for it is particularly in them that we see and meet Christ. (John B. Cobb Jr., *Can Christ be Good News Again?* 49)

"What we do to the poor and oppressed, we do also to Christ—for it is particularly in them we see and meet Christ," so writes John B. Cobb, Jr. All of us are carrying a heavy burden. Even the most affluent of us may be hiding great anxieties and fears and the wounds of our families of origin or guilt over past mistakes. Still, we need to look for Christ in the least likely places, the places where we feel most uncomfortable or the persons with whom we are most distant or alienated. We need, as Mother Teresa of Calcutta counsels, to see Christ in all of his most distressing disguises. This is an act of imagination as well as empathy.

A favorite story of mine involves a conversation between Michelangelo and a curious neighbor. One day, a neighbor observed Michelangelo rolling a boulder up a hilly street to his front porch. Overcome with curiosity when the sculptor began to pound on the boulder, he asked, "What are you doing, hammering on that boulder?" To which Michelangelo replied, "There's an angel inside and I'm trying to let it out." There are angels in boulders, and within an ordinary appearing rock hides a geode.

Christ is present in all things, and all things touch Christ. The least likely realities reveal divinity to those who have senses to intuit. The modern world has lost the sense of the sacred and needs to recover it. We need to rediscover the sacred in osprey, great white sharks, the birds of the air, flowing waters, cats, lions, and the shimmering sea. We need to feel the joy and pain of our human as well as nonhuman life companions.

Christ's universal presence in the world invites us to consider the following questions: Where do you need to look more closely for Christ's presence? What exteriors hide Christ from you? Where do you need to be more attentive to God's pain and joy in experiencing the world?

Affirmative Spirituality

Theological affirmations sensitize us to God's presence in unexpected places. They also enhance our own empathy to the pain and joy of others.

> *I meet Christ in unexpected persons and places.*
> *Christ encounters me in the nonhuman as well as human world.*

Active Spirituality

Consider the unexpected and distressing revelations of Christ. What are the boulders that hide deeper realities of God's presence and care? Take time to reach out with appropriate care to some aspect of life you have overlooked or from which you feel alienated. Seek to bring Christ's presence to this encounter in a way that promotes healing and wholeness.

Praying with Process

Companion of All Creation, wake me up. Give me greater sensitivity to your hidden presence in all things. Help me to go beyond the surfaces of life to experience the holiness of life and then encounter all things with reverence and care. Amen.

 *Day Four*

TRADITION AND INNOVATION

> The function of the Logos is to introduce tension between what has been and what might be and continuously to challenge and upset the established order for the sake of the new.... The one Logos calls persons in different times and places to quite varied forms of realization, each of which is to be transcended in its turn. (John B. Cobb Jr., *Christ in a Pluralistic Age*, 85, 169)

Spiritual stature emerges with the integration of order and novelty, tradition and innovation, and unity and diversity. To the surprise of many who see God as the ultimate proponent of the status quo, Christ is the source of novelty and discontent with the present world and institutional order, including the traditions of our faith communities. Christ is the source of alternative life-giving possibilities for us and the world.

Many people also think of religious faith as promoting homogeneity in terms of belief and practice. Yet the living Christ calls us to "varied forms of realization," appropriate to the transformation of our particular communities. God delights in diversity and works with each community to nurture its own particular gifts for the good of its members and the Earth.

As the source of novelty, God constantly calls us to new possibilities, personally and institutionally. As you reflect on your life and environmental, social, and religious context, where are you experiencing God's call to new life? What will you have to give up to embrace God's novel possibilities? What traditions will you need to affirm to be faithful to God in your place and time? In what ways will you join ancient gifts and future lures in this holy moment?

Affirmative Spirituality

Affirmations present us with provocative possibilities to transform our lives and the world. As you look at your current personal and community setting, awaken to the following affirmations.

> *Christ is constantly calling me to new possibilities of creative transformation.*
> *I let go of outmoded behaviors and traditions and am open to Christ's creative vision.*

Active Spirituality

Contemplation and action are essential companions in creative transformation. Take some time to reflect on the traditions and possibilities of your personal and community life. What traditions and behaviors no longer give life to you and the community? What traditions deserve to be treasured and affirmed? What new possibilities do you need to embody to be faithful to God?

As you are able, begin to live into some new possibilities congruent with your personal and community needs, taking first steps to creative community and personal transformation.

Praying with Process

Ever-living, ever-loving, and ever-adventurous God, we open to the gifts of tradition and the excitement of innovation. We seek guidance in letting go and moving forward to be your faithful companions in healing our communities and the world. Amen.

Day Five
A CHRIST FOR THE COSMOS

> I find myself drawn by Christ into the meeting with Jews and Buddhists and others. In the course of these meetings I must surrender the way I have previously thought about Christ precisely for the sake of knowing Christ better. If it is Christ who is the center, there can be no boundaries. (John B. Cobb Jr., *Can Christ be Good News Again?* 40)

> Christ is the way that excludes no ways. (John B. Cobb Jr., *Christ in a Pluralistic Age*, 22)

As a child growing up in the Baptist church, I often heard people say, "unless you accept Jesus as your personal savior, you will spend an eternity in separation from God." I also heard old-school Roman Catholics claim that "our religion has the fullness of God. There is no salvation outside the church." To my Dad's credit, I never heard my Baptist preacher-father condemn anyone to hell despite the conservatism of the churches he pastored. Nor do forward-thinking Roman Catholics affirm that their church is the foremost and sole vehicle of salvation.

Religion is often used to exclude and marginalize. Often Christ is "bad news" for doubters, agnostics, and persons of other faith traditions. There is another way of understanding God's redemptive activity in Jesus the Christ. Christ reveals God's universal quest for wholeness. Christ accepts and encourages diverse understandings of God and invites us to learn from persons of other faith traditions.

Christ's quest for wholeness embraces every healing path.

As a follower of Jesus, I am open to learning from scientists, environmentalists, artists, poets, critics of religion, and persons from other religious traditions, or from those with no tradition at all. Wherever truth and healing occur, Christ is its source, even if Christ's name remains unspoken.

Affirmative Spirituality

Affirmations open us to the wider worlds of truth and healing. Affirming Christ awakens us to divine wisdom everywhere.

> *I look for Christ's presence in unexpected places.*
> *Wherever truth, healing, and beauty are found, Christ is its*
>   *source.*

Active Spirituality

Find an opportunity today to explore the insights of another faith tradition or a viewpoint with which you are unfamiliar. What truths can you discern in your encounter with this "new" tradition? How might encountering these new truths deepen your faith? How might you integrate these new perspectives with your current faith understandings?

Praying with Process

Loving Mother of us all, whose voice speaks in many dialects and whose wisdom encompasses all the colors of the rainbow, give me an open and attentive spirit. Teach me to listen to the wisdom of others as I share my own insights and wisdom. Let me see my faith as an inspiration to growth and adventure and partnership with persons everywhere. Amen.

Day Six
CHRIST BEYOND CHRISTIANITY

> Whenever we see hospitality, we see the spirit of Christ, thus named or not. The good news is that the spirit of Christ is not reducible to Christians, Christ is more than Christianity. (Jay McDaniel, *Gandhi's Hope*, 5)

The reality we find in Christ is present everywhere, not confined by denomination, creed, doctrine, or sacred space. Though troubling to those who affirm only one pathway to salvation and healing, this is truly good news for all creation, especially those for whom religion has been a source of pain, exclusion, and trauma. It is good news for seekers and agnostics, marginalized persons and the oppressed, people who have been ostracized for reasons of sexual orientation, and persons of other faiths. It is good news for Christians, too. It means that wherever we go Christ is with us. We are never alone or bereft of inspiration. Divine inspiration can come from any quarter, including the nonhuman world.

Let a hundred flowers bloom! Let earth and sky praise God and reveal God's grandeur! Let holy persons of all faiths be partners in healing the Earth!

Wherever we see hospitality, we see the Spirit of Christ. This is good news because, when we give hospitality, Christ's spirit animates and enlivens us. We are Christ-bearers to each other, carrying his healing love to all creation.

Affirmative Spirituality

Opening to Christ's realm of hospitality is a choice as well as a grace. Affirmations remind us to see the world and our place in it with new eyes and to claim our identity as Christ-bearers to the world.

Christ comes to me in every encounter.
I embody Christ in welcoming all God's beloved children.

Active Spirituality

Today, take time to practice simple hospitality in all your encounters. Look for the holy in each interaction. In the spirit of the Benedictine order, treat each person as Christ, regardless of her or his identity, ethnicity, ability, or political persuasion. Pray for the ability to bring healing and wholeness, welcome and acceptance, to each encounter.

Praying with Process

Mirror of Beauty and Love, we see you in every face. We experience your love in the outcast and forgotten and move forward to embrace and heal. Let our arms be wide open to welcome others as you welcome us. Amen.

Day Seven
SPIRIT-CENTERED FAITH

Christian spirituality is the formation of life in response to the divine Spirit that is known in Jesus Christ. The divine Spirit is God. Hence, what we believe about God determines our spirituality. (John B. Cobb Jr., *Can Christ be Good News Again?* 152)

The reality of God's Spirit—the Holy Spirit—is often overlooked in progressive congregations. In the biblical tradition, the Spirit is the intimate presence of God in the human and nonhuman world. In Romans 8, the apostle speaks of God's Spirit moving in creation as well as human life. Creation is groaning seeking wholeness in the transformation of humankind. Deep within us God's Spirit is praying in sighs too deep for words.

God's Spirit is lively, mystical, healing, and unifying. It moves in the depths as well as the heights of our experience. Spirit speaks through the unconscious, through dreams, paranormal experiences, intuitions, ecstatic speech, and experiences of deep connection with God, other humans, and the nonhuman world. What we believe about the Spirit matters and shapes how we experience God in our lives.

Process theology sees the Spirit revealing herself in all things. She is the wisdom of God, enlightening, enlivening, and empowering. Spirit speaks to us in the voices of the nonhuman world and inspires us to unity. Spirit takes us beyond parochialism or speciesism to world loyalty. When we attune ourselves to God's Spirit through prayer and meditation, heart and hands, God's power flows through us to heal creation and bring wholeness to our communities.

Affirmative Spirituality

We are partners with God's Spirit when we look beyond our interests to the well-being of our companions across the dinner table and across the planet. Spirit-sightings can occur anywhere for those whose senses are trained by spiritual practices.

> *The Spirit speaks in me in sighs too deep for words.*
> *I encounter God's Spirit in all creation.*

Active Spirituality

The Spirit is revealed in the groaning of creation and the pain of the nonhuman world. Ask God's Spirit to guide you toward those nonhuman creatures whose voices you are to hear most intimately. One friend in Cape Cod has discovered she has a great commitment to the well-being of opossums. Another friend is committed to planting milkweeds bushes to support the proliferation of monarch butterflies on the Cape. Still another picks up trash on Craigville Beach, near our home, to ensure safety of the seagulls and other species of birds and add beauty to the environment. Act locally to support nonhuman creation in your neighborhood. Think globally to ensure the well-being of species outside your area.

Praying with Process

Spirit of Gentleness, flow through us, enlivening and challenging us to go forward through the wilderness of our time. Give us wisdom and energy to respond to the crises in our midst, caring for the nonhuman world in our neighborhood and for species across the globe. Spirit descend upon us and ascend in us, give life and inspire service to this good Earth. Amen.

 WEEK FOUR

Spiritual Adventures

Religion will not regain its old power until it can face change in the same spirit as does science. Its principles may be eternal, but the expression of these principles requires continual development. (Alfred North Whitehead, *Science and the Modern World*, 189)

WE LIVE IN ADVENTUROUS SPIRITUAL TIMES. Whereas once spirituality was seen as an escape from the world, often taking us away from embodiment and the hardscrabble world of politics and economics, today many people see the spiritual journey as holistic in nature, embracing body, mind, spirit, relationships, and the planet. We are all, as Thomas Merton notes, guilty bystanders who are called by God to immerse ourselves in global transformation as part of our spiritual journeys.

Spirituality has become global in perspective. This involves our affirmation of many spiritual pathways and our willingness to integrate the practices of many faiths into our own spiritual lives.

It also involves developing Earth-oriented, planet-loving spiritual-ities that connect us with Earth as well as Heaven. We rejoice in the earth beneath our feet, the birds of the air, the animals of the ground, and the flowing waters of stream and seashore. We cele-brate divinity in the changing seasons of the Earth as well as in the changing seasons of our lives. In opening to creation, we embrace God's new creation.

Spiritual formation rejoices in the gifts of the past. It honors tra-dition and the spiritual practices of our elders. It also looks forward toward the creation of new practices appropriate to our time and place. Today, we need to join a new monasticism, a commitment to simplicity of life, with deep embodiment, honoring the rhythms of the Earth and our own bodies. Our spiritual embodiments must also inspire us to experience God's presence in the bodies of others, espe-cially the bodies of the oppressed, dispossessed, marginalized, and for-saken. World-loyalty opens us to our unity with all creation, human and non-human alike. In discovering God's presence in ourselves, we recover a sense of reverence for life in all its wonder and variety.

Day One
SOLITUDE AND SPIRITUALITY

Religion is what the individual does with his own solitari-ness.... The great religious conceptions which haunt the imaginations of civilized mankind are scenes of solitariness: Prometheus chained to his rock, Mohamet brooding in the desert, the meditations of the Buddha, the solitary Man on the Cross. It belongs to the depth of the religious spirit to have felt forsaken, even by God. (Alfred North Whitehead, *Religion in the Making,* 16, 19)

We all need time to be alone and to experience our hungers for the Holy. In solitude, the many voices of life, dominating our workdays and relationships, often fade into the background. The Psalmist proclaims, "Be still, and know that I am God" (Psalm 46:10). While God's presence is ubiquitous, and can be found in a crowd as well as a sanctuary, silence is a pathway to experiencing the divine.

> "Go out and stand on the mountain before the Lord, for the Lord is about to pass by." Now there was a great wind, so strong that it was splitting mountains and breaking rocks in pieces before the Lord, but the Lord was not in the wind; and after the wind an earthquake, but the Lord was not in the earthquake; and after the earthquake a fire, but the Lord was not in the fire; and after the fire a sound of sheer silence. When Elijah heard it, he wrapped his face in his mantle and went out and stood at the entrance of the cave. Then there came a voice to him that said, "What are you doing here, Elijah?" (I Kings 19:11–13)

In solitude, the wealth of our experiences may well up. We may feel both desolation and elation, support and abandonment. We may discover with Elijah our answer to the question, "What are you doing here?" That is, what is your calling? What providential purpose is at work in this situation? Your response to God's question may transform your life.

Affirmative Spirituality

Affirmative faith can open us to the deeper dimensions of our experience. We may have to readjust our behaviors and find a healthy blend of contemplation and action.

> *I take time for solitude and stillness to listen for God's voice.*
> *I seek a quiet center from which I can experience new possibilities for healing and service.*

Active Spirituality

Today's quest involves seeking a sacred space and time for solitude. Do you have a sacred space or time? Where do you go to find spiritual nurture? What times of day are most conducive to silence and solitude?

If you don't yet have times or places for prayer, take time to explore ways to create personal rituals for stillness, prayer, and contemplation.

Praying with Process

You are present in our activity, O God, and also in our rest. You are present in our words and also in our silence. In each moment, help us listen for your still, small voice of inspiration and guidance. Amen.

Day Two
BREATHING SPACE

> By spirituality, I mean openness to God's Breathing, day by day, and moment by moment, relative to the circumstances at hand. Understood in this way, spirituality is not supernatural or extraordinary but deeply natural and wholly ordinary. It can be embodied at home and at the workplace, while alone and with others, amid dishwashing and diaper changing, laughing and crying, living and dying. (Jay McDaniel, *Living from the Center*, 3)

On Easter night, Jesus entered the locked room where the disciples were hiding, breathed on them, and said, "Receive the Holy Spirit." Peace is just a breath away. The ordinary activities of going to work, picking up your children or grandchildren from school, reading a bedtime story, or accompanying a senior adult to a doctor's appointment can become windows to the sacred. We can encounter divinity in this perpetually perishing world by making every breath a prayer.

One of my spiritual teachers, Allan Armstrong Hunter taught Claremont School of Theology students a breath prayer, guided by the words,

> I breathe the spirit deeply in
> And blow it gratefully out again.

Buddhist spiritual guide Thich Nhat Hanh breathes prayerfully:

> Breathing in
> I feel calm.
> Breathing out
> I smile.

Our lives are part of a Great Breath, the breath of God giving life to all things. Attuned to this Holy breath, we can breathe our relationship with all creation and experience the grace of interdependence. We can share in the Psalmist's affirmation with every breath: "Let everything that breathes praise God" (Psalm 150:6).

Affirmative Spirituality

Every breath can be a prayer. Every breath can open us to an array of divine possibilities for us and those around us.

> *I breathe in and share God's Spirit with every breath.*
> *I breathe in concert with all creation. Let everything that*
> *breathes, praise God.*

Active Spirituality

Contemplation and action are the yin and yang of the spiritual journey. Process theology encourages "contemplative action" in which our spiritual practices inspire local and global healing, and our political actions deepen our spirituality and connectedness with the whole Earth.

Active spirituality is breathing spirituality. Take time to pause and breathe deeply, inhaling and exhaling throughout the day, saying the following, "I breathe the Spirit deeply in" or "I breathe in concert with all creation." Notice your common breath with all creation, inhaling holiness and peace, and exhaling peace in every situation.

Praying with Process

Breathe on me breath of God, and breathe in me breath of God. Fill me with new life. Inspire me with new energy. Let my breath join the healing breath of all creation, bringing peace to this good Earth. Amen.

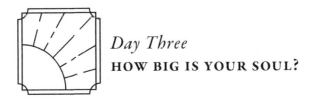

Day Three
HOW BIG IS YOUR SOUL?

By size I mean the stature of a person's soul, the range and depth of his love, his capacity for relationships. I mean the volume of life you can take into your being and still maintain your integrity and individuality, the intensity and variety of outlook you can entertain in the unity of your being without feeling defensive or insecure. I mean the strength of your spirit to encourage others to become freer in the development of their diversity and uniqueness. (Bernard Loomer, "S-I-Z-E is the Measure," Harry James Cargas and Bernard Lee, *Religious Experience and Process Theology*, 70)

Luke's Gospel proclaims that Jesus grew in wisdom and stature. Jesus embraced diversity in all its richness and complexity. He held in tension relationships with groups that hated each other:

Roman oppressors and Jewish freedom fighters, tax collectors and orthodox spiritual leaders, Samaritans and ritualistic Jews, outcasts and insiders. Throughout his ministry, Jesus continued to grow. He shed his people's implicit racism to embrace a Syrophoenician mother; he forgave Roman soldiers for crucifying him; he held out the possibility that Pilate could be redeemed if he opened to deeper truths. Jesus experienced God's revelation in little children, often seen as nuisances in public gatherings, and also in mustard seeds, lilies of the field, and the birds of the air. Jesus found the fullness of God in what John Dominic Crossan describes as a kingdom of nuisances and nobodies.

Today, we need persons of stature, extravagant spirited persons who can embrace political, economic, ethnic, and racial diversity in our increasingly polarizing age. We need to have the largeness of soul to treat our opponents with the same care as we give to those for whom we advocate. We need to commit ourselves to constantly enlarging our spirits, so that no person is foreign and every place is our spiritual home.

Affirmative Spirituality

Largeness of soul is achieved one moment at a time. Stature comes from seeing God in unexpected places. It emerges from the nurture of affirmations that grow our spirits.

> *I embrace God's presence in all its diversity.*
> *I am committed to a lifetime of spiritual, emotional, and*
>   *intellectual growth.*

Active Spirituality

As part of your commitment to growing in stature, reach out to someone whose lifestyle, ethnicity, and beliefs differ greatly from your own. For me, I might attempt to dialogue in a non-polarizing way with a conservative Christian or Tea Party member. Without compromising my own beliefs, I would make it a priority to listen without judgment—to listen with the heart, opening to their deepest fears and hopes—and find common ground in our mutual humanity.

Praying with Process

Give me, O Wise Creator, a soul as large as the universe. Help me live extravagantly and lovingly, looking for your presence in all its many faces and lifestyles. Help every person become a companion and every place become home. Amen.

Day Four
LISTENING FOR THE WORD OF GOD

The image of a universe in process, and even a God in process, has deep implications for Christians who feel called to listen. It means that our process of listening never ceases because there is always more to be heard, to be felt, to be listened to, than has yet been heard. The spiritual life is an ongoing and lifelong process of conversion in which our hearts are continuously transformed by what we hear. (Jay McDaniel, *Gandhi's Hope*, 54)

Frederick Buechner and Parker Palmer capture the two poles of spiritual transformation, "Listen to your life" and "Let your life speak." Gerald May suggests that spiritual practices involve pausing, noticing, opening, yielding and stretching, and responding. First comes the listening—and this listening involves an attentiveness to our deepest personal yearnings and the voices of the world around us, both human and nonhuman. God speaks through our deepest yearnings and the deepest desires of those around us. The art of living the word and wisdom of God in us and in creation involves being still long enough to hear these deeper voices.

We are in deep trouble as communities and persons because of our failure to listen for God's presence in the political, economic, and planetary crises of our time. The prophet Amos predicts a famine of hearing God's word due to our insensitivity to the cries of the poor (Amos 8:11). Hearing is the first step to acting. What is it we need to hear? Where have we been insensitive? Whose pain have we blocked out of our awareness? What does hearing the experience of others demand of us?

Listening joins receptivity and activity and can be part of the justice-making process. We can, in the spirit of Nelle Morton, hear each other into speech. By providing a listening space, others can find their own voices and become our partners in healing dialogue.

Affirmative Spirituality

What we bring to consciousness is often a matter of focus. Among the welter of voices, hearing the voice of God involves taking time to notice and believe that what we notice is important and can change our lives.

> *God speaks to me in all things.*
> *God's voice echoes in the cries of the poor to whom I listen*
>   *with love.*

Active Spiritualty

Listen to your life. Listen to the world. Then let your life speak! As you listen to the deepest voices within, consider toward what actions are you drawn. This could be an inner journey dealing with family of origin issues through beginning a therapeutic relationship. It could be an outer journey of direct or political action through involvement in responding to the needs of the children of the working poor, supporting beach cleanup, or registering your opinion on congressional bills regarding the environment, for example, strip mining or fracking.

Praying with Process

Wisdom Giver, Love Creator, your voice permeates all creation. Your voice wells up in our deepest emotions and thoughts and in our encounters with our human and non-human companion. Help us listen to your Great Life flowing through all things and let our lives speak in acts of compassion and healing. Amen.

Day Five
CONTINUING REVELATION

> Every important revelation, every important incarnation, carries with itself the principle of transcendence. Every revelation exists to be surpassed and therefore every revelation contains within itself a pointing beyond itself. (Bernard Loomer, "S-I-ZE is the Measure," Cargas and Lee, *Religious Experience and Process Theology*, 75)

A Buddhist proverb cautions us to avoid confusing the moon with the finger pointing toward the moon. The moon can't be fully encompassed by human knowledge. There is always something more to be discovered, especially in a dynamic, evolving universe.

The same applies to the reality of any creature and most especially to the reality of a lively, dynamic God. We can never fully know God or another and that's good news. Every creature is mysterious. Each moment contains more connections and hints at more possibilities than we can ever imagine. God's ongoing presence in the universe is beyond any human understanding. We catch a glimpse of divinity, we see God from our perspective, but God is more than we can ever fathom.

Spirituality involves openness to God's continuing revelations. There is no stopping point and the horizons of the Spirit recede toward new horizons with each step we make. We don't need to know everything to be faithful. Within each moment there are insights enough for the next steps in the journey ahead. Each moment—and all creation—is full of divine presence. Reality is never fully understandable, but it is embraceable moment by moment by loving hearts and holy hands.

Affirmative Spirituality

Spiritual affirmations move us forward toward new horizons and inspire us to open to God's new revelations.

> *I open to new horizons of divine revelation.*
> *God's revelations are new every day.*

Active Spirituality

Make a commitment to learning something new in an area outside your expertise. You may wish to discover something about the demographics of your community, the explorations of Pluto, the real experiences of homeless people, the challenges of the working poor, and the impact of global climate change on local flora and fauna. Toward what actions might this new awareness lead you?

Praying with Process

Holy Adventurer, give me a curious mind and a loving heart. Help me to embrace the mystery of life and reverence the holiness of each creature. Amen.

Day Six
ON HAVING A FAT SOUL

In process thought, God is not simply the foundation of order but is also the goad of novelty. Order and novelty are instruments in God's overall aim of creating intensity of harmonious feeling in the universe.... The greater an entity's ability to hold diverse elements of its experience in a harmony of contrast, the greater is its intensity of experience. (Ron Farmer, *Beyond the Impasse,* 114, 124)

In her book in *Fat Soul Fridays*, Patricia Adams Farmer asserts that

a beautiful soul is a large soul, one that can overcome the smallness and pettiness of our human condition. A really fat soul can welcome diverse people, ideas, and ways of being in the world without feeling threatened. A fat soul experiences the intensity of life in its fullness, even the painful side of life, and knows there is something still bigger. (12-13)

Bernard Loomer described such a soul in terms of "S-I-Z-E." He had no interest in theological positions that were small in spirit. Small theologies and spiritualities divide the world into saved and unsaved, welcomed and shunned, and clean and unclean.

In their quest to experience God, Fat Soul spiritual practices look for truth in unexpected places. They welcome divine revelation in a child at play, a monk in saffron robe, a critic of traditional religion, and an elderly adult sharing her life story. They see glimmers of holiness in hammerhead sharks, dolphins, manatee, eagles, iguanas, gold finches, and tigers. In the spirit of Isaiah's mystical experience in the Jerusalem temple, they recognize that the whole earth is filled with God's glory. (Isaiah 6:1-8)

Let your soul grow and your spirit soar. Let your spirit embrace the universe and delight in God's beautiful world.

Spiritual Affirmations

Fat Souls are always open to transformation. They venture out of their comfort zones, open to new images of God and the world.

> *I constantly open to new possibilities and ways of understanding the world.*
> *I embrace revelation wherever it is found.*

Active Spirituality

What aspects of life are most foreign to you? Toward which of these "alien" realities are you most spiritually drawn? Let this be an opportunity to take a first step toward a new world of relationships.

Praying with Process

Soul of the Universe, enlarge my soul. Let my spirit soar with eagles and swim with the whales. Let me know that your energy of love gives us more than we can ask or imagine. Amen.

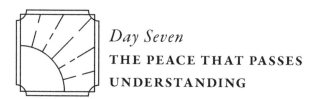

Day Seven
THE PEACE THAT PASSES UNDERSTANDING

Peace is the quality of mind steady in its reliance that fine action is treasured in the nature of things. . . . Peace is self-control at its widest—at the width where the 'self' has been lost and interest has been transferred to coordinations beyond personality. (Alfred North Whitehead, *Adventures of Ideas*, 274,285)

Peace is the gift of transformed vision that liberates us from fixating on the concerns of the moment to see your lives from a larger perspective. This moment and this day are precious and deserve to be savored. Yet, they are part of a much larger adventure in which moment-by-moment experiences are significant. Our lives matter to the universe and to God. Our lives are important, but not all-important, and this is good news. No one moment is ultimate, no one reversal is final; all are part a larger Creative Movement giving life to us and all things. Psalm 8 captures the experience of peace that emerges from the joining of the micro and macro:

> O LORD, OUR SOVEREIGN, how majestic is your name in all the earth!

> You have set your glory above the heavens. Out of the mouths of babes and infantsyou have founded a bulwark because of your foes, to silence the enemy and the avenger. When I look at your heavens, the work of your fingers, the moon and the stars that you have established; what are human beings that you are mindful of them,mortals that you care for them?

> Yet you have made them a little lower than God,and crowned them with glory and honor. You have given them dominion over the works of your hands;you have put all things under their feet, all sheep and oxen,and also the beasts of the field, the birds of the air, and the fish of the sea,whatever passes along the paths of the seas.

> O LORD, OUR SOVEREIGN, how majestic is your name in all the earth!

In the vastness of the universe, we seem insignificant. Yet we have been given a vocation, a task, to be caretakers of the Earth. The term "dominion" is problematic when taken out of context and as a mandate for destruction—when we forget that God is sovereign, the center of the universe and all things, and that our calling is to bring the same care to our activities that God gives to the universe in all its diversity.

Peace is the gift of a larger perspective. It comes from letting go of the self-interested, self-concerned ego and awakening to the movements of the Soul of the Universe. We can face difficulties knowing that nothing can separate us from the love of God and that each moment of our perpetually perishing life is treasured by the God of all Creation.

Spiritual Affirmations

Peace comes from an imaginative vision that joins with all creation and reminds us that our efforts are treasured in God's ongoing holy adventure.

> *My life is part of God's ongoing holy adventure.*
> *My life makes a difference to God.*
> *What I do contributes to the well-being of the universe.*

Active Spirituality

Our lives make a difference to the world and to God. Our acts are like throwing pebbles into a pond; they radiate beyond us to bring greater and love to the world. Small actions can lead to great achievements: so said the teacher Jesus when he described the impact of mustard seeds and fed a multitude from five loaves and two fish. Even a little faith can move a mountain standing in our way. Our planetary healing requires big and bold actions. But the enormity of the crisis can paralyze us until we know that small acts also make a difference. Just a few days ago, I signed a petition to ban the use of plastic bags in Barnstable, Massachusetts, the town in which I live. This is nothing big in and of itself, but it will amount to reducing the use of plastic bags by millions in the years ahead. What small act can you do that can be a catalyst in healing the world? What act of faith can motivate you to become part of something larger than yourself?

Praying with Process

Creative Wisdom, move me to action that heals the Earth. Help me see your calling in my daily tasks and my responsibilities as a citizen. Give me faith to move the mountain of apathy and passivity. Help me find the peace that calms and empowers and trusts your loving power in all things. Amen.

WEEK FIVE

World-Transforming Prayer

> How God answers our prayers is beyond our thoughts, and God's ways are not our ways. But we can trust that our prayers give God more to work with in influencing the world for the good. (Martha Rowlett, *Weaving Prayer in the Tapestry of Life*, 121)

PRAYER IS AT THE HEART of our relationship with God. Prayer is relationship, the ultimate act of connectedness between humanity and God. Theologian Jay McDaniel even suggests that the stars pray as they reflect God's light. The Psalmist rejoices in a world in which snow, sea monsters, birds, and trees praise God. The final verse of the Psalms affirms, "Let everything that breathes praise God." (Psalm 150:6)

Today, science is studying the sacred. Physicians assert that prayer is good medicine and that our prayers can influence the health outcomes of those for whom we pray.

Prayer aligns us with God's vision and aim that we experience abundant life. Prayer inspires activism. Out of our prayers come liberating acts and the recognition that we can be the answer to some-one's prayer by our openness to being God's healing companions.

There is no conflict between contemplation and action. Contemplation centers our spirits, gives us patience and persever-ance, and enables us to see the holiness of those whose behaviors we challenge. We can bless those who curse us and in so doing find common ground with those who initially saw us as their opponents. Prayer is completed when we reach out to others in compassion. As Pope Francis counsels: "You pray for the hungry. Then you feed them. This is how prayer works."

Prayer is incarnational and embodied in healing actions. Prayer creates a field of force around those for whom we pray. Prayer is not omnipotent, but it opens the door to greater infusions of divine energy that can transform cells and souls. It can help us find healing for conditions that cannot be cured.

Prayer changes things. First, it changes those who pray, giving them a wider perspective and transforming enemies into God's beloved children. Second, prayer changes challenging situations. Prayer can be a tipping point between life and death, health and illness, and success and failure. As many preachers have affirmed, "When I pray, coincidences happen. When I don't, they don't."[7]

God hears our prayers. The most moved mover joins our prayers with God's own vision to bring beauty and healing to the world.

Day One
PRAYERFUL INTIMACY

How we think of God affects how we pray...and what we expect our prayers to accomplish. If we pray to a kind of sky god, we are trying to influence some distant and maybe absent being to pay attention to us and act on our behalf. If, instead, we think of God as already here, God isn't above or outside watching what's going on but inside taking part. We don't pray then to get God's attention, but to align our-selves with a presence that is already there. We reach out to and through others to a presence that is already working. We aren't pleading with God to do something God would otherwise be reluctant to do. (John B. Cobb Jr., *Praying with Jennifer,* 65-66)

Prayer awakens us to God's vision for us and those for whom we pray. Prayer is the ultimate act of connection, not limited by space or time. Prayer does not change God's will. God seeks the highest possibilities for each moment of experience and our whole lifetime. God wants all of us to experience abundant life, congruent with our particular past history, relational and environmental context, and the good of the whole.

God is the Holy Here and Holy Now. The One to whom all hearts are open and desires known experiences our prayers as we pray and weaves our prayers into the tapestry of life for us and those for whom we pray. Still our asking creates a field of force that enables God to be more present for our well-being and the well-being of the world.

Spiritual Affirmations

Our affirmations can transform our theology. They enable us to dis-cover an accessible God, as near as our next breath and present in our cells as well as our souls.

> *My prayers open me to God's vision for my life and the healing of the Earth.*
> *God is with me, moving through my prayers to support the well-being of all creation.*

Active Spirituality

God's aim at wholeness moves through all things. God presents us with possibilities for our wholeness and inspires our own lives to support the wholeness of others. In the intricate ecology of life, we can be the answer to someone's prayers. We can undergird another person's well-being. Ask God to open you to God's wisdom and energy. Be open to God's vision for each encounter throughout the day as you seek to be God's companion through your prayers in bringing joy and healing to the lives of others.

Praying with Process

Loving God, to whom all hearts are open and all desires known, inspire us to pray for ourselves and the world. Help us to pray trusting your love for us and those for whom we pray. Weave our prayers with the prayers of the Earth to bring healing to all creation. Amen.

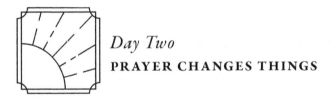

Day Two
PRAYER CHANGES THINGS

> Prayer changes the way the world is, and therefore changes what the world can be. Prayer opens the world to its own transformation. (Marjorie Suchocki, *In God's Presence*, 19)

We live in an open system in which the present and future are not yet decided. What we do today changes the world and provides greater or lesser material with which the Poet of the Universe can work.

When I was a child, my mother affixed a magnet on the refrigerator that announced, "Prayer Changes Things." While she knew nothing about process theology, she expressed the essence of process theology's dynamic, relational world view. Neither God nor our past histories can determine the present and future. In this unique moment, freedom is real. God provides a vision of possibilities and the energy to achieve them; the process of self-creation is up to each occasion of experience.

Prayer opens a channel of blessing for the world and those for whom we pray. When we pray, we toss a pebble into the pool of life, creating ripples of wholeness. Our prayers unite with other prayers—and the desires of others who are praying—to influence the persons for whom we pray.

While our prayers do not determine the outcome of events in a linear fashion, we can still "ask, seek, and knock," trusting our prayers and the future to God's energy of love. Nothing is too large, too small, or too unimportant to God. In a profoundly interdependent universe in which many factors can shape each moment of experience, our prayers can be the tipping point between health and illness, and success and failure, in the situations about which we pray. So, pray boldly. Pray for humans and nonhuman life. Let your prayers be your gift to God and all creation.

Spiritual Affirmations

Prayer changes things. Our prayers and affirmations create a field of force around those for whom we pray. A healthy theology prayer inspires our prayers for others.

> *My prayers bring new energies into the world, aiding the well-being of those persons and institutions for whom I pray.*
> *I pray in every encounter, seeking God's wisdom and bringing new energies to each situation.*

Active Spirituality

For whom do you feel called to pray? In addition to your prayers, what healing actions can you perform to respond directly to your personal prayers? Make a commitment to pray for family members, friends, and strangers as well as political leaders and world situations. Let your prayers take hands to heal the world as they inspire you to embody creative and healthy transformation in your actions.

Praying with Process

Holy One, you hear the cries of creation and our own deepest yearnings. Keep us open to the many ways you come to us, seeking our companionship and challenging us to embody your vision in our relationships. Let your blessings unfold in our lives and in the world, one encounter at a time. Amen.

Day Three
LETTING GO INTO GOD

Prayer in such a world [of relationships with God and others] is an openness to God's own creative energy and to the good that God intends for us. It is also an offering back to God, giving God the gift of ourselves.... Since our prayers are given to God, we must let go of them, trusting God to do with those prayers what God can and will. (Marjorie Suchocki, *In God's Presence*, 28, 34)

Our understanding of what is best for us and others is incomplete and often shaped by our own limited perspectives and self-interest. In an interdependent, dynamic universe, we are encouraged to pray—to ask, seek, and knock—for our deepest needs and the deepest needs of those we love and our world. Prayer focuses our attention on our current desires for ourselves and others. In the focusing, we may—if we are blessed with insight—move from self-interest to world loyalty. Our prayers may become part of the deep prayer of the universe and of God's prayer for and with us.

Ultimately our prayers, however, are our gifts to God. Our prayers share our vision of what is best, then, open us to a Deeper Wisdom and Creativity. Since God wishes us to experience abundant life, congruent with the well-being of others, we can feel comfortable praying and then letting go of the outcome. Metaphysically speaking, letting go is necessary because our prayers are woven together with the prayers of others, our past history, the choices of those for whom we pray, the environment, economic and medical resources, and God's vision. Still, while we can be specific in sharing our desires with God, we must look beyond ourselves trusting with the apostle Paul, that "in all things God is working for good." (Romans 8:28)

Affirmative Spirituality

Affirmations shape our expectations regarding the power of prayer. Our prayers are neither impotent nor omnipotent. They are important, but not all-determining in shaping the future. Moreover, we "see in a mirror dimly," never fully aware of what is best for us or the world. Still we can pray boldly, trusting our lives and the world to a loving God.

> *I pray boldly, trusting God's wisdom with the future.*
> *In all things God is working for good.*

Active Spirituality

Prayer inspires action. As you pray for the world, be attentive to your responsibility to act in a healing way. What one action, accompanying your prayer life, can you make to bring greater healing to the environment? In what ways can you contribute to an ecological civilization by your prayerful activities?

Praying with Process

Deep Wisdom, use our prayers and our lives to bring something beautiful into the world. Let our prayers inspire loving actions in our immediate environment and the world beyond my neighborhood. Amen.

Day Four
PARTNERS IN PRAYER

> Intercessory prayer changes what the world is relative to the one for whom we pray, and that change is for the good.... Prayer for another's well-being allows God to weave us into that other's well-being. (Marjorie Suchocki, *In God's Presence,* 47)

No one fully knows the mechanics of prayer. Often we pray for certain outcomes and appear to fail in our quest for wholeness and transformation. Our prayers appear to be unanswered. Yet prayer is at the heart of the spiritual journey and of our quest to heal the planet. We recognize that, on our own, our efforts will fail. We don't have the will, power, or perseverance. We need a power and wisdom greater than our own to respond to our own personal issues as well as the challenges faced by our family, friends, communities, and the planet.

In an interdependent universe, our prayers matter, even if they are only one factor in the many factors that shape each moment of experience and a lifetime. At the very least, our prayers create a field of healing force around those for whom we pray which may be both preventative and transformative. Our prayers change the world and open the door for God's vision to be more effective in the lives of those for whom we pray.

Fervent prayer makes a difference and requires no prerequisites. Author Anne Lamott describes three types of prayer, all of which can be life-changing: "Wow, thanks, and help." We rejoice in the wonder of the world and our own unique lives. "Radical amazement," as Rabbi Abraham Joshua Heschel asserts, is key to religious experience. We give thanks for the fullness of our lives and existence itself. We praise God for God's goodness, creativity, and love. We plead for help from a power and wisdom greater than our own to complement and enhance our own quests for well-being.

We can never fully understand or discern the impact that prayer makes on our own lives or the lives of others. Surely prayer changes the pray-er and connects us with those for whom we pray. Surely prayer provides an energy of love surround those for whom we pray. In the interdependence of life, prayer can soften hearts, including our own, give us spiritual strength, remind others that they are not alone, and open conduits through which ever-present divine energy may pour.

Walter Wink asserts that the future belongs to the intercessors, to those who join prayers for healing and justice with acts of reconciliation and justice-seeking. Our planetary future is in doubt. The problems we face appear to be beyond our abilities. We can't sit on the sidelines and wait for a divine rescue operation. But we can pray, letting our prayers take wing, letting our hands inspire us to change our lives and to transform the world.

Affirmative Spirituality

Affirmations are positive prayers, describing the most pervasive realities that undergird our spiritual adventures. Affirmations create a space for healing actions for us and others.

> *My prayers create a space for personal and global transformation.*
> *I pray with my heart and act with my hands.*

Active Spirituality

Process theology affirms the unity of contemplation and action, of prayer and politics. Our prayers move us from the sidelines to the frontlines in shaping a better future. What are your deepest concerns today? Toward what realities do they guide you? Pray for insight into one positive action you can commit to and then take the first step in personal, community, and planetary transformation.

Praying with Process

Weave our prayers with the prayers of creation to bring something beautiful to the world. Help me persevere in prayer and out of my prayers let me act wisely to bring healing to myself, others, and the world. Amen.

Day Five
HEALING PRAYER

> Prayers for healing make a difference in what kind of resources God can use as God faithfully touches us with impulses toward our good, given our condition. Those prayers can make the difference between reversing a not-yet-irreversible illness or not; therefore, God bids us to pray. But God only knows the point of that irreversibility, and in some diseases, it is with the very onset.... But what if irreversibility is the case, what then? Shall we stop our prayers for healing? Of course not, for healing comes in many forms, and there is a health that is deeper than death. (Marjorie Suchocki, *In God's Presence*, 58, 60)

Recently a woman came to my study for spiritual counsel. She felt guilty because the texture of her prayers had changed. When her close friend, the spouse of a local pastor, was diagnosed with cancer, she prayed for a cure. For a while her friend's health improved, but then her physical condition plummeted and physicians held out little hope for survival beyond the next few weeks. She was bedridden and drifted between severe pain and a narcotic haze. As she told the story, she confessed, "I don't know what to do. I'm praying for a gentle death, but I feel so guilty. It feels like a want her to die. I simply want her to be free of pain and go to be with Jesus." Her feelings of ambivalence and guilt are not uncommon. When disease appears to be winning, we wonder if we should continue praying or simply give up. What do we do when a cure is no longer possible? Can there be a healing even if there is no cure?

I pray for healing of mind, body, and spirit of others on a daily basis and lead intercessory prayers during public worship services. On occasion, people report cures from health problems and addictive behaviors as a result of our congregation's intercessions. On other occasions, I have prayed fervently for dear friends over several years, first seeking a cure, and then later seeking a spiritual healing when hope for a physical cure was no longer possible.

I believe that there can always be a healing, a transformation of our spirits, regardless of our physical condition. Healing emerges from a sense that God is with us and our lives are in God's hands. Since the mortality rate for life is 100 percent, we all need healing. We need to experience God's spiritual resources when we have reached the end of the road. Yet even then God's love makes a way when there is no way. God provides God's peace, presence, and vision of everlasting life in God's memory and in our ongoing companionship with God.

Pray fervently for a healing. Ask, seek, and knock. Trust that divine energy, wisdom, and love will create a pathway through the valley of the shadow of death and guide us toward the horizons of divine healing.

Affirmative Spirituality

Faith involves a transformed vision of life. Faith sees deeper into reality and discovers God's presence, gently moving to heal us and those for whom we pray, in otherwise desperate situations.

I awaken to God's healing in every situation.
Divine healing occurs even when there is no hope of physical recovery.

Active Spirituality

For whom are you called to pray? Who needs your specific and personal prayers? Take a moment to reach out to that person, if it is appropriate, asking them to share any prayer needs they might have. Share with them your desire to pray daily for them. As you make the commitment to pray, also consider how you can pray with your hands by offering them tangible forms of help.

Praying with Process

Healing Savior, be with us in the challenges of life. Give us a sense of your love and presence. Guide us toward those who need our prayers. Give us healing hands to touch with love. Give us hope that even when a cure can't be found, your healing power is present. Help us trust those for whom we pray and ourselves to your gentle, loving, healing care. Amen.

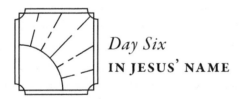

Day Six
IN JESUS' NAME

Christian prayer alters the form or shape of consciousness in terms of which we think and live, and . . . the direction of this change today is global consciousness. Prayer does this when it is done in Jesus' name, that is, when it is not simply a verbalization of what we happen to desire but embodies the transcending and transformation of desire in light of Christ. Prayer understood in this sense cannot be polarized in relation to social action, since its essential character is to reshape the perspective of all thought and action. (John B. Cobb Jr., *Can Christ be Good News Again?* 162)

I grew up singing "All Hail the Power of Jesus' Name." Over the centuries, the name of Jesus has been used to invoke God's presence, channel divine energy to heal the sick, protect people from the forces of evil, and bring peace amid the storm. I learned to pray "in Jesus' name" as a young child and still invoke Jesus' presence in my private and public petitions and intercessions.

The name "Jesus" creates a field of force that enables God to be more fully present to bring wholeness into our lives. When we believe that Jesus is with us in the storms of life, we gain greater courage to continue despite our fears. When we give healing touch in Jesus' name, we access God's ever-present energy of love to bring healing to ourselves and others.

Praying with Jesus takes us beyond the personal to the planetary. Jesus loved the grasses, the lilies of the field, and the birds of the air. Jesus' heart was touched by pain in all its forms. Jesus sought — and still seeks — wholeness for every human and global condition.

We can invoke Jesus' name always and everywhere. We can humbly pray with Jesus as we pound a nail to put up a wall for Habitat for Humanity, advocate for the homeless, support single parents, challenge injustice, and promote policies that heal the Earth. The Galilean healer is present everywhere, bringing healing to every aspect of our lives. Praying in Jesus' name embraces God's wisdom wherever it is found, even when the healer's name is not mentioned. Christ is the way that excludes no ways and embraces all creation!

Spiritual Affirmations

Jesus is God's word of affirmation to creation. When we humbly and hospitably invoke Jesus' name power is released to transform any situation.

> *Jesus brings healing to every situation.*
> *Praying in Jesus' name inspires me to bring healing to all creation.*

Active Spirituality

Jesus challenges us to bring healing to every situation. Jesus is alive and enlivens our hearts and hands to bring wholeness to others. You are the hands and heart of Christ. Make a commitment to use your hands for healing alone. You can do this by learning a healing energy practice like Reiki healing touch; pounding nails with Habitat for Humanity; tutoring children at a local school; circulating petitions to ban plastic bags in your municipality; protesting unsafe environmental conditions. You can pray with your hands and voice as well as your words and heart.

Praying with Process

Healing companion, open my heart and mind. Let your light shine in and through me to bring your healing presence to the world. Thank you for loving us and open us to love one another in Jesus' name. Amen.

Day Seven

COMPANIONS IN CONFESSION

> Prayers of personal confession refer to naming ourselves before God as we truly are, owning to God and to ourselves the harm that we have done to others. The work of naming is at the same time the work of contrition and the release toward transformation that is yet possible for ourselves and others. (Marjorie Suchocki, *In God's Presence*, 67)

One of my favorite scripture passages is Psalm 139. The Psalmist begins the prayer with "O God, you have searched me and known me." The Psalmist takes comfort in the awareness that he or she is fully known by God. Wherever he or she is, God is present — in the heights and depths, light and darkness, far and near. After proclaiming the wonders of God's love and God's nurturing presence, the Psalmist begins to rant:

> O that you would kill the wicked, O God, and that the bloodthirsty would depart from me—those who speak of you maliciously, and lift themselves up against you for evil! Do I not hate those who hate you, O Lord? And do I not loathe those who rise up against you? I hate them with perfect hatred; I count them my enemies.

But then the Psalmist stops and remembers the deep truth of God's presence and confesses once more:

> Search me, O God, and know my heart; test me and know my thoughts. See if there is any wicked way in me,and lead me in the way everlasting.

Confession doesn't provide God with new information. God knows us completely and is aware of both our greatness and our weakness. Confession places our lives in God's care and opens us to God's healing power. Confession reminds us that God knows us completely and loves us completely. In recognizing our fallibility as well as our wonder, we open to God's healing touch, transforming our spirits, emotions, thoughts, and actions, and leading us from ways of death to ways of life.

Spiritual Affirmations

Confession creates new possibilities for personal and planetary transformation. To recognize that you are fully known and fully loved awakens life-changing power.

> *God knows me fully and loves me completely.*
> *Out of my brokenness, I discover the energy to change my life*
> *and the world.*

Active Spirituality

Confession inspires action, both locally and globally. We have much to confess in terms of our destruction of the environment. We have made the Earth a garbage dump and disrespected our Mother, as Pope Francis asserts. We need to confess our complicity in the destruction of the planet, its flora and fauna, and our neglect of the least of these. We need to pray that God creates in us a new heart, open to God's vision for a healed world, as well as the energy to become partners with God. What step can you take to today to move from confession to action? Where have you been neglectful? What life-supporting actions can you commit to for the healing of the Earth?

Praying with Process

Loving God, you have searched us and you know us. You know our greatness and our fallibility; you know when we fall short of your vision and turn our backs on the poor and the vulnerable of the Earth. You know our complicity in destruction of our fellow humans and this good Earth. As we confess our sin, our failure to follow your way, help us to have a new spirit, loving you, O God, by loving your creation. Amen.

WEEK SIX

Healing the World

Since our prayers are given to God, we must let go of them, trusting God to do with those prayers what God can and will. (Marjorie Hewitt Suchocki, *In God's Presence,* 4)

TODAY, OUR PRAYERS NEED TO BE GLOBAL as well as personal. The interdependence of life challenges us to hear the cries of the poor and the groaning of creation. Prayer joins the micro and the macro, the infinitesimal and the infinite, our daily bread and the feeding of millions of malnourished children, our health condition and the health of the ecosystem.

Prayer invites us to do something beautiful for God, grounded in the affirmation that we love the Creator by loving the creatures. As we have done to the "least of these," we do unto God, giving God a beautiful rather than ugly world, minimizing the pain God and creatures experience, and maximizing joy for God and the world.

As I've said before, our prayers can lead to world-changing actions. We can be the answers to God's prayer for the Earth by attending to the well-being of our nonhuman companions and advocating for political changes that reduce our use of fossil fuels, minimize our carbon footprint, and promote the survival of endangered species. We can be the answer to prayers of persons facing challenges of body, mind, spirit, relationships, and economics.

For those who pray, the whole world comes alive. Divinity is discovered in great white sharks and caribou, osprey and lions, milkweed plants, and sea slugs. Prayerfulness opens us to their experiences of joy and pain, and challenges us to affirm the value of the nonhuman world apart from human interests. To pray for creation inspires reverence for life in all its varied expressions. We are ultimately one in spirit, bound together in the fabric of interdependence.

Day One
THE UNIVERSALITY OF VALUE

> A process-relational vision of this world of experience calls us to a wider ethical responsibility toward all creatures. Animals have values for themselves, as well as us. Consequently we have ethical obligations toward them. (C. Robert Mesle, *Process-Relational Philosophy*, 40)

Some people fixate on the chasm between humankind and the nonhuman world. They assume that the command to have "dominion" over the Earth gives us license to objectify and use the nonhuman world as we wish. Sadly this objectification applies to the human world, as well. Some people use workers for profits, neglecting their well-being and stifling their dreams. Nothing, however, could be further from the biblical vision. The creation story in Genesis (1:1–2:4) describes humanity as part of God's lively and evolving world. We are created in the image of God, male and female, with responsibilities to tend the Earth. We are to be gardeners and not destroyers (Genesis 2:15).

The nonhuman world has a personal relationship with God. Meditate on these words from Psalm 148:

> Praise him, sun and moon; praise him, all you shining stars! Praise him, you highest heavens, and you waters above the heavens!
>
> Let them praise the name of the Lord, for he commanded and they were created. He established them forever and ever; he fixed their bounds, which cannot be passed.
>
> Praise the Lord from the earth, you sea monsters and all deeps, fire and hail, snow and frost, stormy wind fulfilling his command!
>
> Mountains and all hills, fruit trees and all cedars! Wild animals and all cattle, creeping things and flying birds!

As Francis of Assisi affirmed, all creatures praise their Creator. Let us raise our voices in praise for God's creativity and in care for all creation. Take a moment to meditate on the hymn inspired by St. Francis' mystical vision:

> All creatures of our God and King, lift up your voices, let us sing: Alleluia, alleluia! Thou burning sun with golden beams, thou silver moon that gently gleams,O praise him, O praise him, Alleluia, alleluia, alleluia!
>
> Thou flowing water, pure and clear, make music for thy Lord to hear, Alleluia, alleluia! Thou fire so masterful and bright, that givest man both warmth and light, O praise him, O praise him, Alleluia, alleluia, alleluia!
>
> Dear mother earth, who day by day unfoldest blessings on our way, O praise him, Alleluia! The flowers and fruits that in thee grow, let them his glory also show. O praise him, O praise him, Alleluia, alleluia, alleluia!

Affirmative Spirituality

Affirmations awaken us to the wonder of life and the value of the nonhuman world apart from interests.

> *I praise God with all creation.*
> *I see the holiness of all life.*

Active Spirituality

We move from praise to action. Our affirmation of creation and the creative wisdom of God challenges us to be Earth-keepers and gardeners of creation. We can initially begin by greater appreciation for our companion animals and the animals in our environment. We can volunteer or support programs that care for abandoned or abused animals. We can also explore legislation and advocacy to promote safe sanctuaries for animals in North America as well as around the world. Most importantly, research about the impact of global climate change on nonhuman life and consider changes in your lifestyle and political commitments to protect the planet.

Praying with Process

Holy One, your voice speaks through all creation. All life begins and ends with you. All nature sings your praises. Help us to sing your praise with each new morning, live gratefully, and honor all creation. Alleluia! Amen.

Day Two
THE ETHICS OF ENJOYMENT

God's creative love extends to all creatures, since all actualities, as experiential, have some degree of enjoyment.

The promotion of enjoyment is God's primary concern throughout the whole process of creative evolution...God wants our enjoyment to be such as to increase the enjoyment of others. To be moral is to actualize oneself in such a way as to maximize the enjoyments of future actualities, insofar as these future enjoyments can be conditioned by one's present decisions. (John Cobb and David Ray Griffin, *Process Theology: An Introductory Exposition*, 36–37)

God wants to promote enjoyment. "To be moral is to actualize oneself in such a way as to maximize the enjoyments of future actualities, insofar as these future enjoyments can be conditioned by one's present decisions." This is not reckless hedonism, but the recognition that morality is about contributing positive experiences to those around us, both human and nonhumans. It is true, as Whitehead says, that life is robbery and sometimes our desires are at cross purposes with the desires of our human and nonhuman companions. Still, our goal should be to promote wholeness of experience and the actualization of positive possibilities for every creature with whom we interact.

Process ethics is profoundly theocentric. As we have done unto the least of these, we do unto God. God experiences our — and other creatures'— enjoyment and pain. At the heart of ethics is the question: Are we giving God a more beautiful or uglier world by our actions? Mother Teresa counsels us to do something beautiful for God, and this is good advice from a process perspective as well. Our lives are our gifts to others and to God. In choosing to bring joy to the world, we honor our Creator and bring beauty to God's life. Today, let us commit ourselves to bringing beauty and healing to every interaction as our gift to God.

Affirmative Spirituality

Affirmations help us live more intentionally and prayerfully. Knowing everything we do contributes to God's experience inspires us to promote beauty and joy in every interaction.

I am doing something beautiful for God in every interaction.
My life is my gift to God. Let it be beautiful.

Active Spirituality

Doing something beautiful for God begins with knowing what brings joy and beauty to those around us. This requires listening to their voices and unspoken words. It involves learning about what brings joy to the nonhuman world. Take time to listen to your companions, human and nonhuman, and, in that listening, to be open to their voices and respond with beauty and love.

Praying with Process

Poet of the Universe, let my life bring an alphabet of beauty to your experience. Let me dedicate my life to beauty and love, honoring all creation in its diversity, and bringing beauty to your life. Let me do something beautiful for you and rejoice in the beauty you give to the world. Amen.

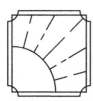

Day Three
THE QUEST FOR BEAUTY

To maximize beauty is to maximize enjoyment. God's purpose, then, can be described as the aim toward maximizing either beauty or enjoyment. (John B. Cobb Jr., and David Ray Griffin, *Process Theology: An Introductory Exposition*, 65)

God aims at beauty and enjoyment for us and for all creation. We are part of a universe that is aimed at beauty and when we are in synch with God's vision, and we can bring beauty to every situation in which we find ourselves.

Process theology affirms the spirit of the Navajo Blessing Way and honors the indigenous peoples' experience of holiness in the nonhuman world:

> In beauty may I walk.
> All day long may I walk.
> Through the returning seasons may I walk.
> On the trail marked with pollen may I walk.
> With grasshoppers about my feet may I walk.
> With dew about my feet may I walk....
> With beauty before me, may I walk.
> With beauty behind me, may I walk.
> With beauty above me, may I walk.
> With beauty below me, may I walk.
> With beauty all around me, may I walk.
> In old age wandering on a trail of beauty, may I walk.
> In old age wandering on a trail of beauty, may I walk.
> It is finished in beauty. It is finished in beauty.

With indigenous peoples, process theology envisages a panexperiential world in which the nonhuman world is alive and able to communicate with humankind. Often we fail to hear the voice of God in the voices of humpbacked whales, osprey chicks, songbirds, coyotes, foxes, spotted owls, and chimpanzees. Our prayer life is a way we "embrace a beautiful God," to quote Patricia Adams Farmer, in all its many manifestations.

When we open our senses to God's presence, we truly walk with beauty and bring forth the beauty in all creation.

Affirmative Spirituality

Opening our senses to beauty is a matter of choice as well as chance. When we commit ourselves to beauty-seeking, the world is transformed. We see beauty everywhere and bring forth beauty wherever it is hidden from the insensitive eyes.

With beauty all around me, I walk.
I see beauty in all things and bring beauty to every creature.

Active Spirituality

Process theologian Patricia Adams Farmer invites us to take "beauty breaks"[8] on a daily basis. I suggest a beauty walk wherever you are. I take a daily beauty walk on Cape Cod beaches. I take a sunrise walk each morning and sometimes leave my study for a five-minute walk to the beach. I also take beauty walks when I am on the road giving seminars and lectures. Even in urban areas, you can experience beauty in scudding clouds, chirping birds, flower baskets, and human and nonhuman faces.

Praying with Process

Beauty-making God, guide us to the pathways of beauty. Help us to see beauty in all things. Help us to experience our own inner beauty and the beauty of our bodies and every other body. Help us to affirm that black lives matter and that all other colors matter as well. Help us to see beauty in every child and in every creature. Amen.

 *Day Four*
REVERENCE FOR LIFE

[In a life-centered ethic] the first moral virtue is reverence for life. This is to have an inward disposition that is respectful of, and caring for, other animals, plants, and the Earth, and refuses to draw a sharp dichotomy between human life and other forms of life. (Jay McDaniel, *Of God and Pelicans*, 72)

One of the best known passages of scripture proclaims, "For God so loved the world." (John 3:16) Notice it doesn't restrict God's love to humankind. God loves the world and that means God cherishes humanity in all its diversity and creativity, as well as insects and birds, sea creatures and lizards—all flora and fauna.

Each creature is of value, regardless of its importance to humankind. Sanctity of life is often used to describe humankind's ultimate value; but process theology expands life's sacredness to embrace the nonhuman world of which we are a part, the nonhuman world that sustains and supports human life.

Humans and nonhumans are intricately related. The threat to polar bears at the Arctic Circle constitutes a threat to humankind. Threats to honeybee populations jeopardize human food production. We all need one another, and our care for the Earth and its many creatures supports our own well-being.

The holiness of life was at the heart of Dame Julian of Norwich's mystical vision of a hazelnut. According to the English mystic:

> And in this God showed me a little thing, a mere hazelnut, lying in the palm of my hand. And it was as round as any ball. I looked upon it with the eye of my understanding, and thought, "What may this be?" And divine wisdom answered, "It is all that is made." I I marveled how it might last, t at its very existence, for I thought it might suddenly fall into nothingness; it was so small. And God gave me wisdom: It exists now and forever, for God loves it. And like the hazelnut, everything has is existence by the love of God." [9]

Reverence for life invites us to affirm nonhuman life by our actions. It challenges us to see the holiness of nonhumans and behave accordingly. When we see life as sacred, we walk in beauty and discover that wherever we are, we are home.

Affirmative Spirituality

Affirmations invite us to behold the holiness of every creature. It is appropriate to see divine wisdom revealed in the experiences of hammerhead sharks, bald eagles, honeybees, cardinals, humming-birds, and monarch butterflies. While the value of life, including human life, is not absolute, our lives are transformed when we look beyond our interests to honor the divinity in all lives.

> *I see holiness in every creature.*
> *I stand in awe before every living thing and treat all things*
>   *with respect and care.*

Active Spirituality

Reverence for life is manifest in an Earth-affirming ethic. This challenges us to live simply and care for nonhuman creatures. Life involves killing, but our killing of animals for food or other pur-poses should be grounded in a sense of gratitude and stewardship. If we eat meat or poultry, we should do our best to consume animals that have been raised in humane ways. We should take special care for endangered species and advocate for the preservation of natural habitats, streams, ponds, and woodlands.

Praying with Process

Loving Creator, your Spirit moves in all things, your heart beats in every creature. We confess our neglect of creation. We have made our world a garbage dump and have wantonly destroyed species. Wake us up to beauty everywhere. Help us claim our vocation as healers of this good Earth. Amen.

Day Five
THE NATURE OF SIN

In a world where God feels the world, all acts or inten-tions that work pain in the world work pain in God as well.

Therefore all sins against the world are sins against God. (Marjorie Hewitt Suchocki, *In God's Presence*, 75)

Once again, we consider the importance of confession for personal and global transformation. Theologian Marjorie Suchocki asserts that "all sins against the world are sins against God." Where have we defaced God's good creation? Where have we destroyed the garden, favoring consumerism over creativity, and greed over beauty? Our worship is empty if our actions destroy human and nonhuman life? Where have we turned away from the lonely and vulnerable? Where have we closed our ears to the cries of the poor?

All of us have much to confess in terms of our interpersonal relationships and care for the nonhuman world, especially those of us living in affluent North America and the developed world. We need to repent, turn around, and move from death to life. We are part of a culture of death, as Pope Francis and some of his predecessors have asserted, and we need to move toward an ecological civilization in which each human and nonhuman life deserves consideration. What do you need to do to choose life our planet today? Where can we be champions of creative transformation?

Affirmative Spirituality

Earth care comes from a transformed way of looking at the world. We repent past behaviors, grounded in values that prize profits over people and consumption over planetary well-being. We can repent, change, and become citizens of an emerging ecological civilization.

> *I turn away from consumerism to value the good Earth.*
> *I train my senses to listen to the cries of creation, and commit*
> *myself to caring for the Earth.*

Active Spirituality

Repentance leads to a transformation of values and changed behaviors. Starting with your current lifestyle, in what ways can you simplify your life? Where do your actions directly or indirectly harm the Earth and its creatures? What first steps can you take to contribute to planetary well-being?

Praying with Process

God of all creation, you speak through creatures of all kinds. Your revelation comes through our human companions and the nonhuman world. Often we forget injustices committed against our brothers and sisters: institutionalized racism, discrimination based on sexual identity, economic inequality; and our nonhuman companions: destruction of habitats, endangerment of species, ravaging of flora and fauna. Wake us up to the beauty of creation that we might walk the earth in simplicity and love. Amen.

Day Six
THE BEAUTY OF HOLINESS

The aesthetic value of life is realized in relation to other individuals and to the cosmos. Moral value is realized in adopting aims for the future that transcend personal advantage. Life is enjoyed as it is lived; but its eventual worth will consist in the contribution it has made to something more enduring than any animal, or than any species of animal. The final beauty is the "beauty of holiness." (Charles Hartshorne, *Creative Synthesis and Philosophic Method*, 321)

"Worship God in the beauty of holiness," proclaims Psalm 96:7 (KJV). Eugene Peterson's *The Message* celebrates our awesome, beautiful Creator.

Bring gifts and celebrate, Bow before the beauty of God,

Then to your knees—everyone worship! (Psalm 96:7)

Worship is about wonder and awe — radical amazement, as Rabbi Abraham Joshua Heschel proclaims. Worship is an ethical act that takes us beyond our narrow self-interest to identify with the well-being of our nonhuman companions. In delighting in God's wise creativity, we are inspired to bring greater beauty to the world beyond ourselves. We are inspired to balance our interests with the flourishing of the planet and its inhabitants. We love God by loving the creatures, and in loving God's creatures, we give our Creator a more beautiful world.

God feels the joy of a soaring eagle and the pain of a seagull caught in plastic netting. God nurtures the migration of monarch butterflies and delights in a child chasing fireflies on a hot August night. God celebrates the love parents and grandparents have for their children and the nurture humpbacks give for their offspring.

A congregation I visited notes in its bulletin, "Enter to worship; go forth to serve." The appropriate service, in our time, is creation care, the honoring of the Earth in all its wondrous diversity. The ethics of worship invite us to delight and care, reverence and nurture, of our own children and the offspring of all creatures.

Affirmative Spirituality

Affirmations open us to the beauty of holiness and our responsibility as creation caregivers.

I bring beauty to every task and encounter.
I worship God by serving creation.

Active Spirituality

As our meditations on the ethics of beauty continue, we continue our commitment to do something beautiful for God. When we love the creature, we love the Creator. With what human companions do we need to share beauty? With what nonhuman companions do we need to share beauty? How can we make our public policy an instrument of beauty and healing?

Praying with Process

Source of beauty, we worship you in the beauty of holiness. We make a commitment to be beauty-makers, bringing beauty to every task and encounter. We love you by loving others and bringing beauty as our gift to you. Amen.

Day Seven
WORLD LOYALTY

Religion is world loyalty. (Alfred North Whitehead, *Religion in the Making,* 59)

Process theology appreciates former Speaker of the House Tip O'Neill's comment, "all politics is local." God is present in the emergence of each occasion of experience, each moment of our lives. God provides possibilities and the energy to achieve them in every moment throughout the course of our lives. Each moment of experience is related to its environment, past, present, and future. Each moment arises from the universe in terms of its immediate and planetary environments, and, dare we say, interstellar environment. Each moment of our lives contributes to the world beyond itself and to God, bringing more or less beauty into the world.

God's vision for each moment joins self-creation with contribution to the world beyond us. Accordingly, altruism is built into the nature of reality. None of us is self-made. We are shaped by the environment of friends, family, communities, nation, planet, as well as the flora and fauna. Apart from a healthy environment, we will perish. All of us make a difference in creating the future.

Whitehead notes that the experience of peace comes from seeing our lives as part of a larger story and balancing our needs with the needs of others, near and far. Peace emerges when we know that what we do contributes to what Brian Swimme and Thomas Berry call the Universe Story and to the Adventure of the Universe, God.

Sadly, politicians and business leaders have focused on individualism rather than on community, and on humankind's economic and military interests rather than the planet's well-being. They have encouraged self-interest, separation, individualism, consumerism, without regard to the well-being of their communities or the planet. Today, we need world-loyalty. We need a larger self-interest that includes the whole planet. We need to see Earth as our Mother, from whom all blessings flow and whose well-being depends on us. We need to foster Earth-centered spiritualities for our technological, global community—spiritual practices that join together our wonder at the natural world with the unrepeatable moments of history. We need to embrace a God who loves lilies and birds, whales and crocodiles, along with human creativity.

Healthy living—authentic family values—takes us beyond self-interest to care for others. This care starts with our own self-creation and then expands to larger and larger circles of loyalty—family, friends, community, nation, planet, and the universe, all embraced by the God of Creative Wisdom. God grieves the pain of parents in Flint, Michigan, whose children have been drinking polluted water; God also grieves the loss of species due to destruction of the Amazon rain forest. God wants all creation to experience abundance appropriate to its environment and ecological niche.

Affirmative Spirituality

World-loyalty finds its inspiration in a transformed consciousness in which we see our creativity connected to the creativity of our planetary companions and our flourishing connected with the flourishing of our human and nonhuman brothers and sisters.

My well-being is connected with planetary health.
My life is my gift to the world.

Active Spirituality

A wise saying goes, "Think globally and act locally." We need to be involved in healing our immediate community through direct action; we also need to advocate on behalf of the whole Earth and its peoples. What ecological and social destruction can you respond to in your local community? What particular need inspires your unique gifts? Looking wider, what global issue touches your spirit? It could be ensuring safe nuclear energy, working to end fracking and strip mining, contributing to programs that protect endangered species, or speaking to your representatives about expanding laws promoting environmental healing.

Praying with Process

Intimate Companion, Lover of All Creation, open my heart and my mind. Take me beyond myself to love the world around me. Help me love my family and friends, caring for them as I care for myself. Inspire me to care for the larger world, caring for other species as I would my own family and friends. Amen.

WEEK SEVEN

New Every Morning

Progress is founded on the experience of discordant feelings. The social value of liberty lies in its production of discords. There are perfections beyond perfections. All realization is finite, and there is no perfection which is the infinitude of all perfections. (Alfred North Whitehead, *Adventures of Ideas*, 257)

GOD IS CONSTANTLY DOING A NEW THING. Faithful through all the seasons of life, God is also actively nurturing new possibilities in companionship with the world. God's visions of yesterday give way to new visions, appropriate for today and tomorrow. While we can cherish past traditions, faithfulness to God involves openness to innovation and novelty. God does not sanction the status quo but invites us to be creative companions in God's holy adventure.

God's call forward joins time and eternity. Although some situations reflect God's vision in unique and energetic ways, all places are potentially "thin places," transparent to God's presence. Miracles, lively manifestations of divine energy, burst forth when we align our lives with God's emerging vision for the Earth.

Our old ways of life are no longer sustainable. Technology alone cannot save us. We need to prayerfully explore technologies that heal the Earth. Personal initiative can no longer be individualistic but must be joined with care for the community and life beyond ourselves. Consumption and production without wisdom destroy the Earth and widen the gap between the rich and the poor. Our survival, and the survival of future generations, depend on novel forms of creativity, sustainable productivity, and energetic actions aimed at promoting planet-friendly agriculture and industry. Our fragile planet demands the interplay of personal initiative and social responsibility in the spirit of Rabbi Hillel's counsel:

> If I am not for myself, who will be?
> If I'm only for myself, what am I?
> If not now, when?

Day One
BEAUTY EVERYWHERE

The teleology of the universe, with its aim at intensity and variety...the teleology of the universe is directed to the production of beauty. (Alfred North Whitehead, *Adventures of Ideas*, 201, 265)

God loves diversity, and God seeks beauty. Creative wisdom, moving persuasively and imaginatively through the universe, brings forth wonders with each new morning. Our cells and souls reflect God's handiwork, and so does the evolution of galaxies and planets.

Variety is said to be the spice of life. It is also the hope of civilization. All the colors of the rainbow reflect divine artistry. The diverse races, ethnicities, cultures, sexual identities, personalities, and gifts enliven the human adventure. The body of Christ, not just the vital church, but also the living planet, has many gifts, all reflections of divine creativity, and all contributing to one another. The flourishing of each creature's gift and each community's vision brings abundant life to the whole.

Let us delight in beauty in all its forms. Delight leads to commitment. We have the power to create beauty through architecture, art, music, worship, technology. We also have the ability to destroy beauty and undermine the beauty-giving structures of our planet. The production of beauty is the gift of the Divine Artist and our own legacy. Beauty is everywhere. You are beautiful. People of all colors are beautiful. Flora and fauna are beautiful. Let us become God's artists of beauty, evolving new forms of beauty along with our creator.

Affirmative Spirituality

Affirmations are the lenses through which we see the world. What we affirm opens us to see the world in new ways, and discover its beauty. Affirmative living brings all the colors of the rainbow to what otherwise might be drab.

> *I delight in diversity.*
> *I see beauty in the varieties of human and nonhuman life.*

Active Spirituality

Spend today delighting in beauty. Train your eye for the beauty inherent in all creation. Say "thank you" to the gifts of beauty coming to you freely, without strings attached. Pause and notice, filled with wonder, the beauty of this moment. Respond with grateful commitment. What one act will bring greater beauty to your neighborhood? What one act will bring greater beauty to persons around you? What one act will bring beauty where it has been defaced by neglect, greed, racism, or prejudice? Let your thoughts take wing to heal the world.

Praying with Process

Beauty-giver, Artist of Creation, for whom all the colors of the rainbow give joy, we have defaced the beauty of our created world, and we have hurt our Mother and put her children at risk. Create in us a delight in beauty for its own sake. Create in us a commitment to be beauty-creators, placing the beauty of others above self-interest. Inspire in us wonder, artistry, healing, and renewal. Amen.

Day Two
THE ONE NEEDFUL THING

> I have come to realize in my years of pondering and praying and philosophizing over both the mundane dailiness of experience and the catastrophic evils of the world that there is only one thing worth all our efforts.... That mysteriously imbedded urge to which we must give ourselves over, wholly, is this: to embrace the beautiful in each moment.... Beauty is that which glistens on the edge of our yearnings and lures us into the depth of things. Its mystery lures us into deep communion with all creation. Its sensuality calls us to incarnate God on our walks on a sandy beach. Its glistening lends buoyancy to heavy days. (Patricia Adams Farmer, *Embracing a Beautiful God,* 1)

What is the one needful thing? What is the one thing that makes life worthwhile? Surely there are many answers to that question. Process theologian Patricia Adams Farmer places beauty at the heart of reality and human aspiration. Opening to beauty involves the quest to incarnate God in all the seasons of life.

Love and justice are connected with beauty. Long ago, the philosopher Plato saw Eros toward the Divine as the inspiration to loving relationships. Inspired by the beauties of this Earth, including the beauty of your beloved, we look toward Beauty that endures through all the changes of life. Love enlarges our spirits and seeks to bring beauty to the lives of our beloveds. Justice also finds its fullness in beauty. We seek justice to promote beauty of experience and to enable others to experience an abundant life that goes beyond mere survival to an appreciation of healthy relationships, to the wonder of creation, and to personal wholeness.

God seeks beauty. The Universe Story can be seen as God's patient quest for beauty in the evolution of galaxies, planets, and persons, as well as in the flora and fauna of our planet.

Process theology counsels us to be beauty seekers and beauty makers. Our gift to others is nurturing experiences of beauty. Beyond experiences of beauty, which are in and of themselves intrinsically valuable, we also shape the planet by creating structures of beauty, communities that promote beauty in human and nonhuman experience, that seek to bring joy to earthly existence in all its variety.

Affirmative Spirituality

Our calling is to seek beauty and then bring it forth in our relationships, personal and political. This involves a commitment to making our own lives beautiful and sharing that beauty with others.

> *I bring beauty to every encounter.*
> *I promote beauty of experience in my life as a citizen.*

Active Spiritualty

Today, begin with one small act of beauty creation — plant a tree, pick up trash on the beach or in a park, read a book to a child, help a child with an art project or a song, write a poem or narrative, bring a smile to another's face. The realm of Beauty emerges one act at a time.

Praying with Process

Source of love and beauty, inspire me to see your artistry everywhere.

Inspire me to make my life beautiful, and out of the materials of my life bring beauty to others. Make beauty of spirit my goal and let beauty flow in and through me in my personal life, relationships, and citizenship. Amen.

Day Three
FAITH BEYOND THE HORIZON

Religion is the vision of something which stands beyond, behind, and within the passing flux of immediate things; something which is real, and yet waiting to be realized; something which is a remote possibility, and yet the greatest of present facts; something that gives meaning to all that passes and yet eludes apprehension; something whose possession is the final good and yet is beyond all reach; something which is the ultimate ideal, and the hopeless quest. (Alfred North Whitehead, *Science and the Modern World*, 191-192)

There is more! If you think you know God fully, then you have created an idol of your own making. The God of the universe is both infinite and infinitesimal, grander than we can imagine, yet embedded in the most apparently insignificant creatures. Indeed, the so-called insignificant is beyond our knowing in its complexity and connectedness.

Faith inspires a holy adventure, guided by wonder and mystery. In this moment, God is fully present. That's the practical meaning of "omnipresence." But, this holy moment reaches beyond itself to the first notes of creation and leans forward to worlds unknown. No creature is fully understandable, but we can lovingly embrace creation in all its mystery. God is never fully understandable, but we can stand in awe of divinity, amazed at God's constant and ubiquitous creativity and love for us and all creation. This awe, wonder, and mystery is the beginning of wisdom and the inspiration of ethics. Reverence and wonder lead to appreciation and affirmation, and to honoring of life in its manifold forms.

Affirmative Spirituality

Wonder and reverence are attitudes toward life. A sense of more, an awareness of the deep mystery of life, emerges with the transformation of our minds.

> *I rejoice in the mysteries of life.*
> *I embrace the unknown, trusting God's presence in all things.*

Active Spirituality

Today, honor the mystery and delight in the wonder of life, by looking more deeply into those you encounter today. It is easy to pass by an insect or child, thinking them unimportant in your journey. Yet, within each creature is the gift of divine creativity and the energy of interconnectedness. Pause and notice, give thanks, and discern how you can honor the mystery of creation. One part of honoring mystery is reverence of subjectivity and appreciation of the uniqueness of each creature. No longer can we objectify, stereotype, or disparage creatures whose realities go beyond our comprehension. We can choose to speak words of appreciation, care, and affirmation, even in the heat of political debate. We can honor otherness as simply part of God's amazing and inscrutable handiwork. Reality is not always understandable, but it is embraceable through loving affirmation.

Praying with Process

Awaken us to the incompleteness of our knowledge, O Mysterious God. Remind us of the partiality and finitude of our vision and the mysterious wonder of life in its abundance. Give us hearts filled with gratitude and reverence, and hands ready to bring beauty to this good Earth. Amen.

Day Four
ADVENTURES OF THE SPIRIT

> The worship of God is not a rule of safety – it is an adventure of the spirit, the flight after the unattainable. The death of religion comes with the repression of the high hope of adventure. (Alfred North Whitehead, *Science and the Modern World*, 192)

When I was a child, adults counseled "safety first." While I practice safety in my own life and daily encourage my young grandchildren to cross the street holding hands, stay a safe distance from the fire when we make s'mores, and be careful coming down the stairs at night, I'm not sure safety is the highest value. In fact, all adventure involves a degree of uncertainty and risk. The ultimate human adventurer once affirmed that those who seek to save their lives will lose them.

Worshipping God is an adventure of the spirit. As the biblical tradition reveals, following God takes us to unexpected places. The cost of discipleship can be personal, spiritual, and intellectual insecurity. It may mean giving up security and safety to bring justice and beauty into the world and to contribute to the healing of another person or a community. Religious faith is adventurous. Just think of Abraham and Sarah leaving everything to follow a dream. Ponder Peter, Andrew, and the Zebedee brothers leaving the security of their family business to follow Jesus. Consider Dietrich Bonhoeffer risking everything to put an end to Nazi atrocities. Imagine Martin Luther King writing "The Letter from the Birmingham Jail" behind bars when he could have secured a professorial position in the North. Imagine everyday women and men leaving secure positions or risking imprisonment to protest injustice or ecological destruction.

Adventures of the spirit take many forms. Each adventure begins with the smallest step — spiritually, intellectually, and politically — and may put us at risk. Yet the risk of love, justice-seeking, peacemaking, and Earth keeping brings beauty to this good Earth and love to the lost and forgotten.

Affirmative Spirituality

Each day brings adventure. Even if you don't leave your home, you can still experience an adventure of ideas. You may also venture forth to horizons of justice seeking. This is an act of trust that the universe treasures our best intentions and brings justice out of sacrifice.

I am God's companion in an adventure of the spirit.
God calls me from the familiar to embark on a holy adventure.

Active Spirituality

Healing the Earth and its creatures lures us on a pathway of adventure. It involves letting go of the stable and familiar to embrace new life. It challenges us to take risks for a greater good. Adventure involves "tragic beauty," and our quest is treasured by God. In what ways might you become part of God's adventure today? What new possibility for personal, social, and planetary transformation lures you forward? What first steps can you take toward adventurous living?

Praying with Process

Adventurous Spirit, give us adventurous spirits. The world awaits those who risk safety to bring justice and healing to the world. The world is desperate for Godward souls who are willing to lose their well-planned and predictable lives to embark on the high hope of adventure. Life and love abound for those who venture toward God's horizons of hope. Let us follow God's adventure, let us embrace God's healing vision, and let us let go of certainty to bring life and light to the world. Amen.

Day Five
ETERNITY AND FLUX

That 'all things flow' is the first vague generalization which the unsystemitized, barely analyzed, intuition of man has produced. It is the theme of some of the best Hebrew poetry in the Psalms; it appears as one of the first generalizations of Greek philosophy in the form of the saying of Heraclitus; amid the later barbarism of Anglo-Saxon thought it reappears in the story of a sparrow flitting through the banqueting hall of the Northumbrian king; and in all stages of civilization its recollection lends its pathos to poetry....

But there is a rival notion, antithetical to the former....The other notion dwells on the permanences in things—the solid earth, the mountains, the stones, the Egyptian pyramids, the spirit of man, God....

Accordingly we find the first two lines of a famous hymn a full expression of the union of the two notions in one integral experience: *Abide with me; / Fast falls the eventide.* (Alfred North Whitehead, *Process and Reality*, 208–209)

Life is a process of perpetual perishing. Each moment, even our most joyous moments, perishes in its immediacy, giving way to the next moment of experience. All things flow, as Heraclitus says. You can't step into the same waters twice, and, perhaps, as one of Heraclitus' upstart disciples noted, you can't even step into the same waters once!

Our lives are brief. We are, as the Hebraic scriptures assert, like the grass, quickly fading. We enjoy our brief lifespan and occupy but a moment in our multi-billion year Earth journey. "Fast falls the eventide." Just yesterday, I was a high school senior, partying at Santa Cruz beach. My friends' parents and my teachers seemed ancient, even though some of them were in their late twenties and early thirties! Their parents were in their late forties and early fifties. Now, I'm in my sixties, a grandparent, and no doubt seem ancient to the participants of our congregation's confirmation class. A few days ago, I spoke with a congregant and planned a get together. The next morning, I received a phone call announcing she had died during the night.

Life passes. The mortality rate remains at 100%. Yet the hymn also notes the enduring realities of life, "Abide with me." The Universe Story and the Creator of All Worlds awaken us to eternity—to everlasting life—amid the passing moments of life. Our lives perish and yet live evermore in God's ever-present, ever-expanding memory. Nothing is lost to the one to whom all hearts are open and all desires known. Everything is preserved, remembered, and treasured by the Most Moved Mover, the One who embraces every moment and all creation in everlasting love.

The Apostle Paul affirms that "love never ends." God's love never ends, and whatever is loved shares in God's everlasting life. This means all creation, in its imperfection, finitude, and cross-purposes.

The good news is: Delight in the now. Celebrate the temporary. Seize the moment to add to the beauty of the Earth. This is the day that God has made, let us rejoice and be glad in it. Trust in tomorrow. Your life matters. Your life is part of God's never-ending holy adventure.

Affirmative Spirituality

Our spiritual affirmations can root perpetual perishing in God's everlasting life. They inspire us to seize the day, knowing that today's adventures contribute to God's everlasting life and radiate back to the world in healing ways.

> *I celebrate each moment, treasuring each moment as an opportunity to bring love and beauty to the world.*
> *Each moment of my life is part of God's never-ending adventure.*

Active Spirituality

Make each moment count. Toward what horizons is God calling you in this one wild and precious moment? What is the gift of each moment today and tomorrow? What loving act can you do today as a partner in God's new creation? Take a chance, risk adventure and wonder by reaching out.

Praying with Process

God of changing seasons, novelty, and change, we celebrate each passing moment. Each moment is a holy moment, filled with possibilities for adventurous living and loving. Remind us that "this is the day," this day is holy, and calls us to seize the moment to bring healing and beauty to the Earth and its creatures. Amen.

Day Six
EVERYDAY SALVATION

A postmodern womanist theology understands salvation as an activity, as a kind of changing. The quest for wholeness, health, freedom, and justice involves a combination of God's activity in revealing possibilities that affirm God's vision of the world and the agency of the world....Salvation is universal in that all human beings, living things, and non-living things, may experience it. Still salvation is particular and contextual for each of us, each situation, and each community in the world....We are being saved over and over again, feeling God's continual calling toward survival, justice, and quality of life, using each opportunity to become in higher and more intense forms than we did in the last occasion. (Monica A. Coleman, *Making a Way Out of No Way*, 95, 169)

The story is told of the encounter of Yale professor Hal Luccock with a street corner evangelist. As the professor walked past him, the evangelist, eager to tell a sinner about salvation, asked, "Are you saved?" To which Luccock responded, "Every day."

Process theology sees salvation, or wholeness, as a universal, moment-by-moment, lifelong, and everlasting process. The quest for wholeness is universal. God constantly provides each moment of experience a vision of what it can be and the energy to achieve that vision. For the most part, we fall short of God's vision for our lives. We may give up on ourselves. Dominated by shame and guilt, or marginalized by oppressors, we may come to believe we are unworthy of God's love. But, God never gives up on us. God's love is relentless. God's love is also intimate and personal. Not framed in terms of a generic "four spiritual laws of salvation" or a homogenous "path to salvation," God addresses each one of us uniquely. We are, as process theologian Monica Coleman proclaims, "being saved over and over again."

As I child, I heard the Billy Graham theme song, "Just as I Am," and its call to come to God without pretense and with all our doubt and sin. Process theology makes the same claim: God comes to us personally, providing us what we need to be whole. Yet, unlike the individualistic approach characteristic of Billy Graham's crusades, process theology sees salvation as involving the totality of our lives, political, economic, ethnic, sexual, family of origin, and planetary. God's quest invites us to become "saved persons in safe communities and a healthy planet."

Salvation involves affirming the uniqueness of each person. If this moment is holy to God, then it must be holy to us. A saved soul must be treated with reverence. A saved soul deserves safe streets, clean air, and adequate food and housing. If God loves her, then we are called to love as well.

Salvation is a process in which we go from grace to grace and light to light. We are, as John Wesley preached, called to lives of holiness, wholeness, and sanctification. Growing closer to God

enables God to present us with greater possibilities and new ener-
gies of wholeness. Yes, we are saved every moment as we open to the
wonders of God's love for us.

Spiritual Affirmations

Affirmations awaken us to God's universal and moment-to-moment
saving grace. They enable us to intuit God working in the lives of
those around us and to see each person as a revelation of God to us.

> *I am being healed moment by moment.*
> *God's salvation opens me to new horizons of grace and justice.*

Active Spirituality

Social gospel prophet Walter Rauschenbusch once stated that "Hell's
Kitchen [a New York ghetto] is not a safe place for saved souls!" This
could easily apply to the environments of many of our human and
nonhuman companions. Looking just at the human condition, much
of the human community lives in dangerous neighborhoods, lacks
sufficient food and clean water, has substandard housing, and faces
economic and political uncertainty and violence on a daily basis. The
problems are so enormous that we are tempted to shut down emo-
tionally. However, as Jewish mystics and process theologians both
affirm: when you save one soul—or moment of experience—you
save the world. What is the most pressing need for children and
families in your community? What threatens the well-being of saved
souls in your area? What one thing can you or your congregation do
as a first step to creative transformation?

We need to act locally, but we also need to think globally. What
global situation inspires you to action? What one activity—financial,
political advocacy—can you participate in as a first step?

Praying with Process

Your love, O God, is personal and immediate. You provide a vision
of possibilities and healing energy sufficient for each moment. Your

love embraces and enlivens all creation. Open us to your quest for salvation in our immediate neighborhood and across the globe. Give us energy and creativity to be your companions in saving the world. Amen.

Day Seven
TRAGIC BEAUTY

> At the heart of the nature of things, there are always the dream of youth and the harvest of tragedy. The Adventure of the Universe starts with the dream and reaps tragic beauty. This is the secret of the union of Zest with Peace — that the suffering attains its end in a Harmony of Harmonies. The immediate experience of this Final Fact, with its union of Youth and Tragedy, is the sense of Peace. In this way the world receives its persuasion towards such possibilities as are possible for its diverse individual occasions. (Alfred North Whitehead, *Adventures in Ideas*, 296)

I spend virtually every afternoon with my two young grandchildren. Their imaginations are boundless. Their dreams are almost unlimited as they create worlds populated with sharks, dolphins, and Lego toys. As a young man, growing up during the "summer of love," I imagined a new world order, a new age in which the swords were beaten into plowshares and nations forsook the ways of war. Too soon many of my baby boomer generation were caught up in the world of their parents, lured by the dream of prosperity and possession. The dream of youth was compromised by realism and consumerism: Walden Pond gave way to BMWs, Zen Buddhism to hurry sickness, and meandering pilgrimages to 24/7 communication technology. The limitless horizons of the summer of love morphed into unlimited consumer opportunities, living beyond our means, junk bonds, and instant gratification.

My generation of North American boomers has been complicit in destroying the world of redwoods and seashores that were so alluring in the salad days of the anti-war and counterculture movements.

Life begins with the dream, and one can pray that my baby boomer generation will reap the harvest of "tragic beauty." Tragic beauty involves the interplay of idealism and realism, of going off to the far country, losing our direction, and then finding our way home by a different path. The path we need today is the interplay of youth and tragedy, the redemption of consumerism and ecological destruction, of self-centeredness and instant gratification, motivated by the vision of a new Heaven and a new Earth. We need an ethic of beautiful sustainability.

There are no guarantees that we will change our ways. Global climate change is transforming the polar ice caps and changing weather patterns on Cape Cod and Laguna Beach. The gap between the rich and poor is increasing, and the middle class is losing its sense of confidence in the future, often succumbing to individualistic politics that see every immigrant as an enemy and job taker.

Most days I feel on the verge of hopelessness about the future and the life ahead for my grandchildren. But then hope emerges — not false or unrealistic hope, but the deeper realism that comes from discovering God in the darkness and recognizing that amid the valley of the shadow God is our companion.

Still, there is the hope that we will experience "tragic beauty," repent of our destructive lifestyles, and become midwives of an ecological civilization. We can experience peace amid the storm, even the storms of our own creation, by knowing that we are not alone. God's wisdom guides us toward horizons of hope and creative transformation.

Affirmative Spirituality

The hope of beauty amid tragedy involves a transformed consciousness. Healing vision moves us from alienation to unity, and destruction to new creation.

> *I trust God's vision of wholeness and beauty amid the challenges of life.*
> *I see the world and myself with hope. I trust the future to God's care.*

Active Spirituality

Life begins with the dream of youth. Yet, dreams are often lost, and we succumb to an unimaginative realism. Still, we can dream again. We can imagine an alternative reality. We can visualize a beautiful planet and humanity transformed; we can experience the dream of Shalom in difficult times. Pause and take some time to dream of an ecological civilization. What images of the future awaken you each morning? What hopes energize you? What first steps can you take to move from tragedy to beauty—for yourself and for our planet?

Praying with Process

Holy One, give us hope. Holy Adventure, give us a glimpse of another world. Holy Life-giver, awaken us to a new vocation as Earth Healers. Confident that we can change, let us risk taking new directions, sacrificing destructive ways of life for our great-grandchildren's futures. Let our wealth be relational and spiritual. Let our treasure be the beauty of holiness and the transformations of the spirit. Grant us peace that passes understanding and faith that moves mountains and changes weather patterns. Amen.

# A FINAL WORD

The Adventure Continues

An insistent craving — the insistent craving that zest for existence be refreshed by the everpresent, unfading importance of our immediate actions, which perish and yet live evermore. (Alfred North Whitehead, *Process and Reality,* 351)

THERE ARE SOME PEOPLE who are so heavenly minded that they are no earthly good. There are also others who are so earth bound that they have no sense of the Spirit. Process theology embraces the spirit of Jesus' prayer "your kingdom come, your will be done on earth, as it is in heaven." Heaven on Earth, holiness in the every day, and everlasting life amid perpetual perishing — this is the vision that energizes our hopes and inspires us to persevere as healers of the Earth.

This world presents enough challenges that we need not worry about life after death. If we are faithful to our calling in this lifetime, eternity will take care of itself. Still, we can imagine a never-ending adventure in companionship with God's own holy adventure. We can imagine that the beauties and challenges of this lifetime are part of a Greater Life that zestfully joins beauty and tragedy.

As a pastor, my vocation involves caring for the dying and providing comfort for families at the hour of death. I have come to believe that physical death is not the end of our human adventure. There is something more awaiting us and our loved ones. I believe that love never ends and that God's love completes what is unfinished, heals what is broken, and restores what is lost in the course of our lifetimes. I believe that the starving child will find refreshment and companionship around a table where there is enough for all. Our companion animals will be reunited with loving humans and abused pets will experience the joy of loving homes. We who see in the mirror of life dimly will come to the world through the eyes of love, fully experiencing the mind of Christ.

Traditional images of reincarnation and heaven and hell are too individualistic. The afterlife isn't about "me." It is about "us"—all of us! It's about the transformation of all things—this world and the next—in God's loving heart.

There is an Afterlife Adventure we can imagine. We can envision life in a community of love and healing, where all sin is forgiven, forgiveness and restoration is the norm, and every creature grows toward wholeness. Tragedy is transformed into beauty, lost memory restored, and abundant life the hope of all creation.

We can barely see the landscape of God's future for us and all creation. We can pray that the process continues in our never-ending Adventure with God and all creation. Life begins with prayer and at the end of the day our prayers find wholeness in God's everlasting Adventure. So we conclude our journey with a prayer for this moment and eternity, committing our lives and the world to God's everlasting love and awakening to the tasks of transformation toward which we are called today.

Praying with Process

Amid the passing of time, of life's perpetual perishing, and Earth's precarious future, give us hope for today and tomorrow. Let us trust that our lives matter and that our acts make a difference in the future of our planet. Let us lean toward God's everlasting vision and the hope of life everlasting. Let us find eternity in perpetual perishing and hope in finitude, for you are the Holy Adventure that dries every tear and embraces every creature now and forevermore. Amen.

RESOURCES
FOR SPIRITUAL
TRANSFORMATION

Books Cited

Harry James Cargas and Bernard Lee, *Religious Experience and Process Theology.* Mahweh, NJ: Paulist Press. 1976.

John B. Cobb Jr., *God and the World.* Eugene, OR: Wipf and Stock, 2000.

John B. Cobb Jr., *Can Christ be Good News Again?* St. Louis: Chalice Press, 1991.

John B. Cobb Jr., *Christ in a Pluralistic Age.* Philadelphia: Westminister, 1975.

John B. Cobb Jr., *Praying with Jennifer.* Eugene, OR: Wipf and Stock, 2004.

John B. Cobb Jr. and David Ray Griffin, *Process Theology: An Introductory Exposition.* Philadelphia: Westminster, 1976.

Monica A. Coleman, *Making a Way Out of No Way: A Womanist Theology.* Minneapolis: Fortress Press, 2008.

Patricia Adams Farmer, *Embracing a Beautiful God.* St. Louis: Chalice Press, 2003.

Patricia Adams Farmer, *Fat Soul Fridays,* CreateSpace, 2013.

Ronald Farmer, *Beyond the Impasse: The Promise of a Process Hermeneutic.* Macon, GA: Mercer University Press, 1998.

Thich Nhat Hanh, *Be Still and Know: Living Reflections on Buddha and Christ.* New York, NY: Riverhead Books, 1996.

Charles Hartshorne. *Creative Synthesis and Philosophic Method.* LaSalle, IL: Open Court, 1970.

Julian of Norwich, *The Showings of Julian of Norwich,* translated by Mirabai Starr, Charlottesville, VA: Hampton Roads, 2013.

Catherine Keller, *On the Mystery: Discerning Divinity in Process.* Minneapolis: Fortress Press, 2008.

Jay McDaniel, *Gandhi's Hope.* New York: Orbis, 2005.

Jay McDaniel, *Living from the Center.* St. Louis: Chalice Press, 2000.

Jay McDaniel, *Of God and Pelicans.* Louisville: Westminster/John Knox, 1989.

C. Robert Mesle, *Process-Relational Philosophy.* Templeton Press, 2008.

Thomas Oord, *The Nature of Love: A Theology.* St. Louis: Chalice Press, 2010.

Martha Rowlett, *Weaving Prayer in the Tapestry of Life.* Bloomington, IN: WestBow Press, 2013.

Marjorie Hewitt Suchocki, *In God's Presence.* St. Louis: Chalice Press, 1996.

Alfred North Whitehead, *Adventures of Ideas.* New York: Free Press, 1967.

Alfred North Whitehead, *Process and Reality,* corrected edition, Donald Sherburne and David Ray Griffin, eds. New York: Free Press, 1979.

Alfred North Whitehead, *Religion in the Making.* Cambridge: Cambridge University Press, 2011.

Alfred North Whitehead. *Science and the Modern World.* New York: Free Press, 1997.

SELECTED BOOKS ON PROCESS
SPIRITUALITY BY BRUCE EPPERLY

Emerging Process: Adventurous Theology for a Missional Church. Cleveland, TN: Parson's Porch Books, 2012.

God's Touch: Faith, Wholeness, and the Healing Miracles of Jesus. Louisville: Westminster/John Knox, 2001.

Healing Marks: Healing and Spirituality in Mark's Gospel. Gonazales, FL: Energion Publications, 2014.

Holy Adventure: 41 Days of Audacious Living. Second Edition. Cleveland, TN: Parson's Porch Books, 2014.

The Power of Affirmative Faith. St. Louis: Chalice, 2001.

Process Theology: Embracing Adventure with God. Gonzales, FL: Energion Publications, 2014.

Process Theology: A Guide for the Perplexed. New York: Continuum, 2011.

Reiki Healing Touch and the Way of Jesus. Kelowna, BC: Northstone Books, 2005.

Tending to the Holy: The Practice of the Presence of God in Ministry. Herndon, VA: Alban Institute, 2009.

ENDNOTES

1   John B. Cobb, Jr., *God and the World* (Eugene, OR: Wipf and Stock), 43.

2   Thich Nhat Hanh, *Be Still and Know: Living Reflections on Buddha and Christ* (New York, NY: Riverhead Books, 1996).

3   Thomas Oord, *The Nature of Love: A Theology* (St. Louis: Chalice Press, 2010), 2.

4   Charles Hartshorne, *Creative Synthesis and Philosophic Method* (LaSalle, IL: Open Court Publishing, 1970), 12.

5   Alfred North Whitehead, *Process and Reality,* corrected edition, Donald Sherburne and David Ray Griffin, eds. (New York: The Free Press, 1978), 244.

6   Whitehead, *Process and Reality,* 105.

7   Quotation widely attributed to 17th century British statesman Sir William Temple. Social reformers of the day reportedly prayed daily for three hours and encouraged Christians to do the same when critical debates were held in parliament. When critics told Temple that answered prayer was no more than coincidence, this was his rejoinder.

8   Patricia Adams Farmer, *Embracing a Beautiful God* (St. Louis: Chalice Press, 2003).2.

9   Julian of Norwich, The Showings of Julian of Norwich, translated by Mirabai Starr. (Charlottesville, VA: Hampton Roads, 2013), 13–14.